SURVIVE YOUR PROMOTION!

THE 90 DAY SUCCESS PLAN FOR NEW MANAGERS

Katy Tynan

Personal Focus Press
Hudson, Massachusetts

http://www.personalfocuscoaching.com
http://www.surviveyourpromotion.com

Printed in the United States of America
First Printing: February, 2010

ISBN: 978-0-615-34463-8

Acknowledgements

This book is dedicated to the many wonderful managers, mentors and leaders with whom I have had the privilege of working over the years. I am profoundly grateful to my parents who support me in all of my projects and my son who teaches me that risks are worth taking. To the members of the Thrive Networks team, thank you for putting up with me as I learned all of the lessons in this book the hard way.

Contents

SURVIVE YOUR PROMOTION!

Introduction

It's a big moment. You've been waiting, planning and pushing to make the transition from the cubicle to the corner office. Maybe you wanted to make more money, have more responsibility or be able to prove to your family and friends that you've truly made it in your career. So you've put your pictures on your new desk, and sat in your new chair – now what? How do you figure out what to do in your office now that you've made it there?

If you're lucky, you have a mentor – someone you know (ideally someone in your field) who can give you some tips. If you're truly fortunate your company will invest in some training or coaching so you can get off on the right foot. But for many people it's a matter of reading books, asking questions, and trying not to look stupid in front of the team.

This book is here to help get you through the critical first 90 days of your new career in management. In my consulting career I had a chance to see the inner workings of hundreds of companies, and to work with managers from every industry in addition to managing my own team. I learned some great lessons about what works and what doesn't and saw patterns emerge as I observed managers who were truly successful.

In this book you will find all of the information you need to get started; with clear explanations of terms and a practical resource guide to point you in the right direction for further study and learning. We'll go through everything you need to do to adapt to your new role by breaking management down into five key functional areas:

Motivation – In this section we will talk through the daily life of a manager, and review what your company expects from someone in your position. We will also discuss the motivation of your team members (individually and collectively) and your role in keeping them focused and moving toward their goals.

Mindset – Shifting your mindset from an individual contributor to a team leader takes conscious effort. In this section we will examine what has changed, and how to approach your new responsibilities. We'll talk about some practical strategies for leveraging your time, and how to avoid some of the pitfalls many new managers confront.

Method – After your promotion you will be inundated with new responsibilities, and you'll need a strategic plan to keep things from falling through the cracks. The Method section will give you a targeted, specific action plan that you can apply in the first 90 days to make sure you are moving in the right direction.

Measurement – Business management is a science and as such you will need to familiarize yourself with the tools and processes by which results are measured. You need to understand how you are being evaluated by upper management, how to track the progress of your team, and how to monitor your own growth and effectiveness. In this section we will discuss some common terminology used in business measurement, and make sure you know how to align your team's goals with the goals of the organization.

Momentum – Once you have gotten the first 90 days under your belt, you will want to keep your career on track. In this section you will learn ways to keep your focus, deal with conflict, manage meetings efficiently, and find tools and resources to overcome the inevitable challenges that will arise as you progress up the ladder in management.

Within this book you will also learn about some commonly used management tools, acronyms and analysis strategies. Familiarizing yourself with the tools and terminology that you are likely to encounter as you go about your daily tasks in management is vital to your success. If you attend a management meeting and they refer to a SWOT analysis or SMART goals, you don't want to be frantically searching the internet on your mobile device under the table. You need to have a handle on what these tools are, how they are used, and how they might apply to your team.

As part of your ongoing personal development, you will also need to stay current with the various trends and tools that other managers are using. In the Resources section of the book I have listed a few "must read" books including commonly used business and leadership titles you are likely to hear mentioned when you interact with experienced managers. In addition you will find web sites and other contact information for time management and leadership training solutions, employee relations resources and sources for information on communication style and personality assessments.

So get yourself a cup of coffee and settle in. The next few months are likely to be hectic, and the sooner you become familiar with the roadmap for your transition from individual contributor to leader, the more likely you are to be successful in your new career.

PART 1

MOTIVATION

CHAPTER 1

What Makes a Great Manager?

If you ask a bunch of elementary school kids what they want to be when they grow up, I'll bet that not one will have "manager" on the list. Yet once you get started in your career you, like many others, may find that you aspire to be a manager.

People list many reasons for why they want to move up the corporate ladder. Some common goals are:

- Make More Money
- Have More Responsibility
- Be In Charge

In the next four chapters we will explore some common motivations for becoming a manager, and discuss how to uncover your company's reasons for putting you in this management role. We will review the motivations of the individual contributors on your team, how they relate to your success as a manager, and finally, we will talk about building a team culture and encouraging your staff to work together. Let's start by talking about the daily life of a manager.

For many the expectation of what a supervisory job will be like and the reality of day to day life as a team leader or manager are quite different. You may make more money, and you will certainly have more responsibility, but you will also have a whole new skill set to master. You will be responsible for work that is not your own, but you will not (unless you have been promoted to Owner) have much more control than you had as an individual contributor.

Am I saying that a promotion is a bad thing? Absolutely not! Moving up to management is a great thing for many people, and can have terrific benefits for you personally and professionally. It is simply a substantial change from the life of a team member, and you need to be prepared to make that change in order to be successful. Let's review some of the common activities that make up a manger's day:

Working as part of a Team

A management position is a leadership role. This may seem obvious, but it's surprising how many people who are perfectly happy working solo find themselves profoundly unhappy when they have to collaborate, build consensus, and generally spend all day relating to people. While there will certainly be times when you work alone as a manager, the vast majority of your new role will involve collaboration with your team and colleagues.

If you are frustrated or unhappy when you have to work with others to get things done, you should think twice (or more) about taking on a management role. There are very few environments these days that will allow you to act as a dictator – you will need to function collaboratively in order to succeed.

Leading Meetings

Regardless of your industry or department, meetings will become a large part of your daily life as you transition into a management role. Not only will you be responsible for facilitating and making presentations to your own team, but you will also have to speak up and participate in meetings with your colleagues and the management of your company as a whole.

If you would rather die in a fire than speak in public, you will want to get that out of your system as soon as possible. Fortunately there is training available to help even the most reticent individual learn the skills to speak up in front of a group. See the Resources section for some recommendations.

Teaching and Mentoring

As we will discuss in the Mindset section, many leaders are promoted because they are the best individual contributors in their department. If this applies in your situation, it means that you are probably more skilled than the individuals you are now managing.

Some new managers find it frustrating when their team is unable to perform at the same level they are used to demanding from themselves. Your new goal will be to transition your mindset into that of a teacher and mentor. You can do that by developing individualized plans for each member of your team and supporting them as they grow their skills.

What this means in practice is that you will need to be patient. If you succumb to the temptation of doing the work yourself rather than helping someone else figure out how to get it done, you will find that you are buried in tactical work and are not getting the strategic aspects of your management job done.

Advocating for Your Team

In contrast to the previous scenario, you may have been hired to manage a department of people who have very deep technical knowledge, and who want to (or have to, due to their lack of management skills,) remain individual contributors. This is very common in the technology industry. Software developers, network managers and specialized technical folks frequently report to managers who do not have their depth of technical skill.

In this scenario the manager is often in the position of being an advocate for his or her team. As the representative of your department to the organization as a whole, you act as the liaison between the technical people on your team and the management team members. To be successful in this role you will need to truly enjoy delving into esoteric subjects and then learning how to translate them into business terms.

Communicating

Much of the ad-hoc communication in today's business environment takes place via e-mail. In one of my management positions I routinely received over 300 e-mails per day. I had a team of 10 engineers who worked in the field, and we made most of our important day to day decisions through electronic communication tools such as e-mail and IM (Instant Messaging).

Successful leaders and managers enjoy communicating with people in every possible form and venue. From face to face meetings to extended written reports, you will need to do more than just go through the motions of polite discourse. To maintain the balance between team productivity, upper management goals and customer needs, you will need to truly understand a wide variety of people with differing communication styles and adapt your style to make yourself understood.

Many successful managers are students of interpersonal communication. They learn to watch for facial expressions and variances in body language, as well as understanding the nuances of electronic communication. They constantly seek out new ways of improving their own ability to communicate with others.

Solving Problems

If you're the type of person who hates change and gets frustrated or thrown off when things don't go as planned, you may not enjoy your management role. One of the aspects of a management job is to support your team members' ability to focus on their own work. New edicts come down the pipe from upper management and customers change their minds about what they want. Someone will always want your team to drop everything and do something for them instead of focusing on the priorities you have in place.

As the manager, your role will be to insulate your team from these disruptions by acting as a mediator and gatekeeper. Minor changes can and should flow around you but anytime someone wants to re-arrange your team's priorities, they will need to come to your door to do it.

One of the benefits of this situation is that you will have new challenges every day. Management is rarely boring because just when you get the hang of it, someone will throw you a curve ball. If that's what you like, you will probably be very happy in your new role, but if change and distraction stresses you out, you will need to work on being more adaptable to be successful.

BUILDING ON YOUR STRENGTHS

If you read the previous section and feel like you are ready to take on your new responsibilities, your next step is to take an inventory of your personal strengths and evaluate what motivates you. As an individual contributor, your manager likely presented you with either positive or negative reinforcement on a regular basis which motivated you to get your job done right. Once you become a manager you will need to motivate yourself as well as your team. In addition you will need to consider (and remember) why you wanted to be a manager in the first place.

The old saying goes, "when you're up to your neck in alligators, it's hard to remember that you went in to drain the swamp." Having a clear picture of why you want to take on this new role, and what skills you bring to the table can be important when you run into challenges later on. Typically your personal motivation falls into two categories:

1. Things You Seek to Gain
2. Things You Want to Avoid

Examples of the first category include things like new responsibilities or more money. The second might be work that you find uninteresting or unchallenging, a management scenario you dislike or a working environment that fails to stimulate your creativity.

No matter what is driving you to seek a promotion, you need to understand the factors that are pushing you to make a change. Why? Because the more clearly you define what makes you happy in a job, the better you are to be able to determine whether or not a specific job is a good fit for you. Maximizing your potential for success involves knowing what you enjoy doing, what you are good at doing, and evaluating what skills you need to work on to be more successful.

A great exercise for any new manager is a personal SWOT (Strengths, Weaknesses, Opportunities and Threats) analysis. You can use it to evaluate what you bring to your new job, and where you need to focus your personal development time and efforts to ensure your success.

On the following page you will see the SWOT framework with questions for each section. Take a blank sheet of paper and brainstorm as many answers for each section as you can. Feel free to contact your friends, co-workers and mentors and ask them what items they might add.

Completing this analysis can help you get a more thorough picture of what you bring to the table as an employee and a manager. Consider developing a plan for each weakness and/or threat and use this analysis as a jumping off point for conversations with your manager about training and personal development. We will revisit this analysis in the Personal Development Plan section of Chapter 5.

At this point you should have a good picture of the daily life and priorities of a manager, and what strengths and weaknesses you bring to that role. In the next chapter we will move on to discussing what your company wants and needs from you, and how to understand what you need to do to be successful.

Table 1 - SWOT Analysis

SWOT Analysis Template	
Strengths	**Weaknesses**
• What do you do better than anyone else? • What would you consider your greatest talent? • What accomplishment are you most proud of? • Name something at work you can do very easily that others struggle with.	• What tasks do you avoid at work? • What do you find most frustrating? • Name something you have tried to do several times without success. • List times where you have had to ask for help with a task.
Opportunities	**Threats**
• What parts of your industry are growing? • What does your organization do better than your competitors? • What technology could make you more effective/efficient? • What training would you love to attend?	• What obstacles are preventing you from achieving your goals? • Do you feel you are at a competitive disadvantage? • What limitations do you have that put your career at risk? • What personal issues could impact your job performance?

CHAPTER 2

What Your Employer Wants From You

While it's important to know why you want to be promoted, it's critical to understand why your organization is promoting (or hiring) you. Employment is a two way street, after all. You are getting paid to do something in which you are skilled, experienced, and enjoy. Your company is hiring you to achieve specific organizational goals.

In most companies the process of creating a new position involves a complex cost justification which clearly states the monetary value that the firm expects to reap from that role. In order for you to be successful integrating yourself into your new job, you need to understand why your position exists at all.

Whether your role is newly created or you are stepping into an existing job, your organization has expectations for your output and the output of your team. Understanding what upper management (from your direct supervisor all the way up to the CEO) wants from you will help you define the goals and objectives of your team.

In the case of individual contributors, the value to the organization is usually quite obvious. For example a magazine publishing company requires a certain number of writers and editors in order to produce the content they need to print a magazine each week or month. Each hire is based on the capacity of the individual to produce a certain amount of work in a set period of time. That work can then be translated into revenue by dividing (as an example) the number of articles per magazine by the amount of revenue earned by that publication.

The ROI (Return on Investment) calculation for a manger can be more complex. It is assumed that a manager is going to organize and facilitate a team of individual contributors. A manager's contribution is usually measured by looking at the cost of the team as a whole in relation to the output or value that the team brings to the organization.

No matter how you came to be in your position, your ability to be successful in it will depend on how well you fulfill the expectations that upper management has for you. So how do you determine what those expectations are? Here are some ways to uncover the details of what's important to your company.

1. **The Job Description** – The very first place to check for key information about your priorities is your position description. A well written example will include metrics for success or other key performance indicators (KPIs) for which you will

be held accountable. Make sure you pay close attention to each phrase or metric since they are often carefully worded and relate directly to measurable goals for your team and your personal productivity.

2. **Your Boss** – As part of the interview process, you most likely received some information about the qualities your immediate supervisor was looking for in hiring for this position. In the first 90 days, you should plan to meet regularly with her or him to review your goals and build a productive working relationship. By using active listening skills and techniques, you will be able to collect a wealth of useful information about what your boss values in an employee, and what you can do to maximize your potential for success.

3. **Other Managers** – Within your organization, and possibly within your department, there will be other people in supervisory roles. You will also encounter other managers and supervisors in the course of your daily operations. Building relationships with your peers can help you more fully understand the culture of the company as a whole. You will see patterns emerge in the behavior of the more successful team leaders working around you that you can emulate to

4. **Industry Groups** – Many fields have networking groups that meet on a formal or informal basis. Joining one (or several) of these is a great way to

expand your personal network. These groups can be an excellent resource where you can gain perspective on the working environments and priorities of your peers. You can also get ideas and tips on how to solve problems that others have already encountered, allowing you to avoid mistakes and learn strategies to be more effective.

Understanding your employer's needs is an important aspect of your success. Hopefully you have taken on a position for which your skills and experiences are a good match, and you share the values of the organization as a whole. This will make it easier for you to adapt your style to your specific environment. Regardless of whether or not you agree with every aspect of your organization as a whole, you must at a minimum understand what you need to do in order to be perceived as successful by your manager.

CHAPTER 3

Motivating Individuals

In Chapter 4 we will talk about building a team and developing a culture that encourages people to be their best. Teamwork and culture are rooted in the motivation and satisfaction of the individual members of your team. So before you can work on your team, you need to understand the motivations of each person who reports to you.

Sigmund Freud believed that people are inherently lazy and will do nothing if not motivated through a clear reward/punishment strategy. This is the old carrot and stick method, and while it is a rudimentary way of getting people to do what you want them to do, it is not always the best route to accomplish your goals. If you use this method you can expect that people will adhere to the letter of the law, but it's unlikely you will build a creative atmosphere.

Abraham Maslow, another noted psychologist, had the opposite position from Freud. His view was that people, given the opportunity, will strive to be their best. Maslow's theory implies that if you hire a great team and create a culture that encourages people to be successful, they will rise to the occasion because that's what they truly want. If you were able to hire an entire team of self directed, highly self-motivated people, simply standing back and allowing them to do their best work would seem like an ideal scenario for a manager. Unfortunately it's rare to have all of your team members functioning at that level.

In practice it is likely that you will need to draw a little from each theory as you work with specific individuals and scenarios. While it's important to have clear consequences for some behaviors (such as adhering to company policies), you should also focus on building a culture that rewards creative thinking and new initiatives to support and retain your high performers.

When I analyze how I feel about any job I take, I rate it on the following five factors:

> **Opportunity to Learn New Skills** – Does this position give me the chance to be trained in and exposed to knowledge, tools and resources that will help me become more successful? This is a highly rated factor in the IT industry, for example, since an individual's ability to earn more money or enhance their job security is closely tied to their repertoire of certifications and skills.

> **Opportunity to Advance my Career** – Is there room for me to grow my responsibility set or evolve into a higher level of management within this organization? Are the things I am learning and doing here going to help me to be more marketable outside of this organization?

> **Level of Stress** – Is the level of stress that I will encounter in this position consistent with my ability to perform at my best? Some people work better under pressure, others don't.

> **Money** – Am I earning a competitive wage for the work that I'm doing and is there an opportunity to earn more than my salary if I do exceptional work?

> **People** – Am I surrounded by individuals I respect and with whom I enjoy working, and do I have good relationships with my colleagues?

Individuals will prioritize these factors differently, and their perception of how their job fulfills each one of them contributes to how they feel about their work as a whole.

One of the first exercises I typically do with a newly hired team member is to ask them to rank the list above according to their own priorities and tell me a little bit about how each one relates to them personally. I like to hear examples of scenarios where they have felt that a job does or doesn't fulfill one of these key five factors. If I find someone who ranks Opportunity to Learn New

Things at the top of their list, I make sure that we focus on their training and development. Similarly someone who is highly motivated by Money will need a competitive salary and bonus structure.

No job provides 100% satisfaction across all five factors, and you will not find an individual who weighs each of the factors equally. But this exercise can be a great tool to help you and your employee develop a plan to incorporate aspects of their strongest motivating factors into their goals and daily activities. This focus will ultimately increase their overall job satisfaction.

This can also be a good exercise to use with an employee that seems to be unhappy or de-motivated as well. An individual's motivation is not static, so you will want to revisit their motivating factors if you see a major change in their performance. Let's break it down with a real world example.

Kevin originally took a job working at a local hardware store because the people with whom he worked were great and the stress level was low. He loved helping people find what they needed in the store, and unlike his previous position as a sales representative, he didn't have to work long hours. When he left at the end of the day, his job stayed at work and he could go home and spend time with his wife and kids.

Last week he found out that his wife (a Human Resources Manager) was being downsized and would be out of work in 6 weeks. Suddenly money and opportunity for advancement became much higher on his scale of motivating factors. Ideally, Kevin would come to you as his manager and let you know about this new development. Depending on his perception of the opportunity for change within the organization, he might just go out and look for another job.

Active listening is a key management skill and, combined with an effective goal planning process, is the foundation of individual motivation. Your ability to build a relationship that encourages your team members to come to you when they feel unmotivated or have life changes that affect their performance will relate closely to your ability to retain your highest performers. We will revisit these concepts throughout the book and discuss more ways of building and reinforcing your relationship with your team members.

Figure 1 – Factors that Effect Individual Motivation

The five factors listed in Figure 1 are all aspects of motivation. They apply specifically to how your team members feel about doing their jobs. In addition you will need to consider is whether they have the tools to succeed. A person can be highly motivated and want very much to do their job, but if they are unable to do it due to lack of skills, training or support, they (and you) will be unable to achieve the goals of their position. To determine where an individual stands in terms of their ability and willingness to do their job, you can use the Employee Motivation Matrix which is shown in Table 2. This framework can help you understand and resolve the root cause of motivation-based issues, and apply solutions appropriately.

Some people will overstate their skills and abilities while others will understate them. As a manager it is your challenge to determine either in the hiring process or based on an observation of their work to date, whether your team members are sufficiently able to perform the work that is asked of them. You can find the answers to this question in a variety of ways:

1. **Observation** – A great way to find out how confident and competent an individual is at a task is to watch them do it. In the interview process you can ask them to show you a sample of their work or to demonstrate how they would solve a particular problem. On the job you can sit in or observe your team while they are actively engaged in doing work.

2. **Credentials** – In many industries specific credentials are required in order to obtain a position. You can ensure that your team members have the credentials and prior training required to do the work that is specified in their job responsibilities by requesting their application materials or copies of their certifications from the Human Resources Department.

3. **Interviewing** – When you take on the position of manager or team leader you may be responsible for building a team from scratch or you may inherit one that already exists. Either way you should sit down with each individual (or candidate) in an interview-style setting and talk through their work experience. Using a combination of active listening and questioning, you can establish how much they know and where they might have weaknesses. It can be useful to have each team member perform the personal SWOT analysis discussed in Chapter 2.

While the motivation matrix is not the only way to view your employees, it can be a helpful exercise to determine where you need to apply time and resources to help each person to operate at their peak.

You will not be able to complete this exercise until you get to know each person on your team and observe how they handle the work they are assigned, how they approach their job, and how they respond to critiques and obstacles that come their way. However, it is worthwhile to begin with this framework in mind so you can utilize the information it provides as you begin to develop a working relationship with your team.

Table 2 - Employee Motivation Matrix

	WILLING ← → UNWILLING	
ABLE ↑	**Can/Will** • Provide training and opportunities to grow their skills • Watch for burn out • Focus on the results and not the process – give them room to figure out the best way to accomplish a task	**Can/Won't** • Have a 1 on 1 conversation to uncover what motivates them • Create a structured plan with the team member to move towards a higher level of motivation • Watch for turnover if there is no way to adapt the situation
↓ **UNABLE**	**Can't/Will** • Partner employees in this quadrant with those in the quadrant above as a mentoring relationship or provide coaching yourself • Provide a structured plan to grow their skills • Watch out for asking for too much responsibility too fast – these employees will always be reaching beyond their limits – don't let them set themselves up for failure	**Can't/Won't** • Avoid pouring resources into an employee in this quadrant as they may not be a fit for the position and you will get a better return on your investment developing employees in the other quadrants • Evaluate whether this team members job can be restructured/adapted or whether another position is available which offers a better fit

Be aware that lack of capacity will tend to degrade both ability and willingness. By this I mean that even a highly skilled, highly motivated individual will tend to be frustrated, make mistakes, and ultimately become burned out if they are constantly overscheduled or asked to do more work than they are able to complete. If your skilled staff members are unable to produce high quality work due to time constraints, they will quickly become de-motivated.

CHAPTER 4

Building a Great Team

I n addition to understanding what you want from
your job, what your employer wants from you, and
how each individual on your team is motivated, your
larger goal will be to build a cohesive team. One of
the reasons that managers exist is to facilitate teamwork
in order to accomplish goals that individuals could not
complete by themselves.

A group of happy, high performing individuals is not
a team. Even if each of the people who report directly to
you is highly motivated and wants to do great work, you
will still need to spend time actively developing a sense
of unity and collaboration in order to foster a true team
oriented environment. Many managers make the mistake
of assuming that just because people are working in the

same space or on the same projects it makes them a team by definition. Working in parallel with others is not the same as being mutually supportive and dependent on one another.

Building a team takes time – you can't expect to complete it during your first 90 days or even your first year. In this chapter we will review the building blocks of a team environment, so that you can work on this aspect of your role over time.

Successful teams have some common attributes that you can encourage and foster as you interact with the members of your group. You will need to model these values through your actions as well as your words. Articulating them to the individuals in your group is a great first step toward developing a team oriented culture.

Trust

All effective teams operate on a foundation of trust. Whether you have participated in team sports, or have only known of teamwork in your professional life, you are probably familiar with the concept that the whole team should be greater than the sum of its parts. This principle (actually called "Gestalt theory") summarizes the concept that each individual member of the team brings certain skills and abilities which, when combined, make the whole team better.

Of all the objectives in this book, building trust among the members of your team will take the longest. Trust is based on pattern recognition. Each person on your team needs to see consistent behavior patterns from you and their colleagues over time in order to be able to believe that a certain person will act a certain way. You can jumpstart the trust building process from day one by committing to the following principles:

1. **If You Don't Know Say So** – If your team members know that you won't make things up, and you will admit to what you don't know, they will be more likely to believe what you say when you do claim to know the answer and will rely on your word.

2. **Limit Your Emotional Volatility** – While it might feel good to vent, if you act like the sky is falling all the time, your group will refrain from telling you when there are problems, and you will come across as unstable. Keep your emotions in check and if you must blow off steam, do it outside of the office.

3. **Keep Your Promises** – If you make a commitment, stick to it. If you can't, communicate the change quickly and clearly. The more often you back down from commitments, the more you will erode your team's trust.

4. **Insist on Respectful Communication** – Like a parent at the dinner table, you are responsible for maintaining a standard of professionalism in the verbal and written communication within your group. Be clear that you expect and encourage

healthy debate, but personal attacks or inappropriate comments will not be tolerated.

While building trust is a long term process, the benefits of having a trust relationship among your team members are substantial. In the Resources section I recommend Patrick Lencioni's book, *The Five Dysfunctions of a Team*, which clearly articulates trust as the foundation of productive working relationships.

Open Communication

A healthy team will have debates, sometimes even heated arguments. While having these conversations can be great for your team's creativity, you want to ensure that they remain within the boundaries of respectful communication. Challenging another team member's assertion can help refine an idea and make it more marketable. Coming up with multiple solutions to a problem can get it solved more quickly and efficiently. You will need to mediate these debates to ensure that they stay on track, and you should encourage everyone to contribute to the discussion.

In addition to endorsing open communications in meetings and among team members, you should have an open door policy for yourself. Regardless of how much you have on your own plate, you need to practice the discipline of putting it aside and being open to hearing from your team members if and when they need your time. You can always place boundaries on this policy if a particular employee is over-using your availability, but that's generally the exception rather than the rule.

Being available to your staff for questions, brainstorming sessions, and acting as a sounding board will encourage them to keep you in the loop on issues. Make sure you approach these conversations with positive energy and focus on using active listening and questioning skills.

Mutually Supportive Goals

Later in the Method section we will discuss the process of setting and tracking goals for individuals and for the team as a whole. As you do this, you should be mindful that if you want your team to work together and support one another, their goals should be in alignment and one person's goals should never be in conflict with another's.

Your aim is to encourage your team members to work together where it makes sense, and to share information. If the success of one person undermines another person's ability to reach their own objectives, they will not be inclined to help their team-mate. It's your responsibility to review everyone's goals and determine whether there are any conflicts.

TEAM BUILDING EXERCISES

At some point in your career you probably had to participate in an artificial teambuilding exercise. Everyone dreads these sessions and while they sometimes turn out to be fun, it's debatable whether they actually have any effect on the formation of a cohesive team. I'm not going to recommend that you hold hands and sing songs. Unless you want your staff to run for the hills, your initial steps towards encouraging teamwork should be a bit more subtle.

1. **Friday AM Snack Meeting** - Have a weekly or monthly team meeting on a Friday morning around 10AM. Don't make it too early or it will become a chore – let people get in and read their emails first. Have a light agenda and suggest that anyone who's got a difficult issue they are working through can bring it to the group for a quick brainstorming session. If no one offers anything, put something out there yourself and let people offer suggestions and ideas.

2. **The Buddy System** – If you have some individuals on your team who are experienced and others who are newer to the field, set up a buddy system where the veterans each have someone to mentor. The more senior person can do the heavy lifting on big projects and then let the less experienced person help out with some of the easier bits. This way you expose the junior members of your staff to more complex projects, and you allow the senior members to develop mentoring and management skills themselves.

3. **Recognition** – When you see examples of teamwork going on in your group, make sure you recognize them. A quick email letting a team member know that you noticed and appreciated his or her effort to help someone else goes a long

way. You don't have to stop the presses and ring a bell, just let your staff know that you are aware of what they do, and that you notice when they help each other out.

4. **Ask for Input** – New managers often think that asking for opinions is a sign of weakness. In reality the opposite is often true. While you shouldn't make every decision a team event, keep your eye out for issues where their input would be valuable, and then ask for it in a structured manner. Send out an email or put an item on a meeting agenda and solicit your team members' opinions. Let them know that you are considering an issue, that their input is valuable, and that you'd like to hear their thoughts before you make a choice that will impact them. If anything this will build you up as a leader, not make you look weak.

Building a team is a slow process. It won't happen overnight and there may be some setbacks along the way. If you keep your focus on creating an environment where everyone is working toward the same larger goals, and where you encourage and reward collaboration, teamwork will grow over time.

MOTIVATION WRAP-UP

Your success as a manager is contingent on your ability to clearly understand these four key concepts relating to individual and team motivation.

1. Be clear about your own motivation in seeking a management role, and realistic about your own strengths and weaknesses as they relate to the skills required to be a great manager.

2. Understand the expectations that your company and your manager have of you in this role. Make sure you understand your own value so you can manage from a position of strength.

3. Uncover what drives each member of your team to be their best and foster an environment of high performance and creativity whenever possible.

4. Build a culture of teamwork based on open, respectful communication and trust.

If you can achieve these goals, you will be well on your way to building a cohesive team and being a great leader.

PART 2

MINDSET

CHAPTER 5

Shifting Your Focus

The role of a manager is fundamentally different from the role of an individual contributor. It requires you to change how you think about your job, what you do on a daily and weekly basis, and most importantly, how far ahead you think. As a manager you not only will need to have a solid handle on what your team is doing this week, but also be planning for goals that are over the horizon by weeks or even months. Transitioning to this longer term view takes practice. In this chapter we will review some tools and concepts to help you adjust your focus.

People often believe when they are promoted to a management position that they are going to "tell people what to do". In truth, a more accurate description of a manager's role would be the breaking down of larger initiatives into individual goals and targets, and the facilitation of the completion of those tasks to bring the larger initiatives to completion.

In order to accomplish both of those tasks effectively, you will need to develop two different but related skills. Management is the act of breaking down the larger initiatives into their component tasks. Leadership is the process by which you will encourage and inspire your team members to achieve those goals.

LEADERSHIP AND MANAGEMENT

At a fundamental level, a leader is a person who motivates others to behave in a certain way. Leadership books and seminars almost always focus on the practice of inspiring action. In the previous section we discussed motivation at length, and by learning how to motivate your team members and fostering a team environment you are practicing the art of leadership. In short, a leader is someone who makes the people around him or her operate at a higher level.

A manager is more likely to be described as an organizer, a process builder and a decision maker. Managers facilitate activities which ultimately produce results. They focus on processes and deliverables (specific items or results to be produced), and find ways to remove or avoid any obstacles to success. This book is a practical guide to management which contains some tangible processes that will also make you a better leader. In the Resources section I have identified some books and seminars which can help you evolve your leadership skills as well. In the first 90 days of a new management position, keeping your focus on mastering the tactical process of management will lead you to a stable state from which you can evolve your leadership style over time.

The difference between telling people what to do and managing or leading them to success can be boiled down to the concept of responsibility. As a manager and leader your success is indistinguishable from the success of the team. You are responsible for facilitating positive results across multiple individuals. This concept of responsibility for the work of others requires a shift in mindset.

RESPONSIBILITY

In transitioning from a team member to a manager, you are shifting into a mode of being held responsible for work that is not your own. Since it is likely you were promoted to management in part because of the high quality of your own work, the team you are being asked to manage is probably comprised of individuals who are less skilled or motivated than you are. Your new responsibility, therefore, is to raise the level of your team's work through developing your staff.

This shift puts you squarely in the position of mentor and coach. In Chapter 1, I talked about evaluating your team members' abilities to perform work that is assigned to them, and I introduced you to the Can/Will Can't/Won't framework. Once you have identified an area where a particular team member needs development, you can create a plan to coach them through learning these new skills. The best thing you can do to prime yourself for success as a team leader is to create a development path for each member of your team which will move them towards producing high quality work. It can be challenging to watch someone make mistakes, and the temptation to just take over and do it for them will always be present. However, if you take the reins and do the work yourself, you will lose the opportunity to build up the skills of your team members, which is your ultimate the road to success as a manager. Here are some specific things you can do to mentor your team members and build up their skills:

> **Provide Resources** – Mentoring and coaching can be as simple as pointing someone in the right direction. Instead of giving someone the whole answer, point them towards the next step and see how far they get.

> **Review Work** – If a team member is putting together data for a presentation to a larger group, and they don't feel 100% confident about their work, offer to review it when it's 80% complete and provide suggestion and direction on what's missing.

> **Offer a Sample** – If you can cite an example showing what you or someone else did in a similar situation, you can demonstrate the process and the final result without actually stepping in and doing the work. This can give your team

member a clear guideline for what you expect to see that they can use as a template.

➢ **Be Available** – If a member of your team is working on something under a deadline or at a client site and you know that they are not 100% confident in their ability to complete it success-fully, make yourself available by phone/email until the task is complete. Sometimes just knowing that help is there if they need it can give an individual the confidence to get the job done themselves.

Being responsible for the overall output of your team is a substantial challenge. There will be times when you are not satisfied with the results that someone else produces. As long as your focus is on their development, and how you can help them work towards improving the quality of their work, you will be focused on the right goal.

THE CURRENCY OF LEADERSHIP

How you are viewed by your team, your colleagues, your customers and your own management is the next mindset adjustment. In the past you were judged by the quality of your work, but as a manager your ability to develop relationships will depend on an entirely different currency.

As an individual contributor, your primary method of adding value to your organization was the quality and quantity of your work. While your ability to work as a team member and support others was a great bonus, most companies would keep you on board as a highly talented, productive worker without great communication skills or any leadership potential. As a manager you are valued for something completely different.

In a leadership role, your word is your primary currency with your team members, your colleagues and your customers. If you commit to getting something done for any of these constituencies, you must get it done or lose the credibility that is fundamental to your success. Many new managers slip into the bad habit of over-committing. They promise too much, set unrealistic deadlines, and fail to properly plan for obstacles and contingencies.

To succeed in the early months after your promotion, make sure you are mindful of all commitments you make. Keep careful track of deadlines. If you are asked to estimate the time required to complete a project, ask for time to put together a full analysis before you commit to a timeline. As you refine your knowledge of your team and their capabilities, you can start to make off the cuff estimates, but when you are just getting started it's far better not to guess.

Keeping your word is the first step in building trust – the essential ingredient for productive relationships with your team members, colleagues and customers. Trust takes time to develop – there is no magic formula for generating it overnight. However there are some fundamental behaviors that you can practice to build trust in all of your business relationships.

➢ **Be Consistent** – Trust is, at a basic level, pattern recognition. If you are calm and patient one day and running around shouting the next, you will erode people's trust in you. That's not to say you should be a drone with no personality, but rather that you should moderate your responses to the ups and downs of your working life.

➢ **Don't Over Commit** – It's tempting to say that you will have something done the next day when you know that's what someone wants to hear. If you can't deliver on it you will be constantly backpedaling. That behavior will quickly mark you as unreliable and recovering from that poor reputation will be difficult.

➢ **Keep Confidences Confidential** – As a manager you will be privy to information that is not available to everyone. Whether the information comes from your team or from upper management, if you commit to keeping a confidence you must do so. You will have to use your judgment if you believe that keeping a confidence represents a danger to an individual or the organization as a whole. As a basic rule, if someone asks you to keep something private, it should remain between the two of you.

➢ **Be Fair Minded** – Life is not fair. It's not possible to create a work environment where everything is fair either. However you should keep fairness in mind in your work relationships. Don't give preferential treatment to someone who is your friend outside of work. Avoid conflicts of interest whenever possible, and use your own moral compass to advise you when you are considering the fundamental fairness of an action.

> **Tell the Truth** – If you don't know something, admit it and move on. If you make a mistake, own up to it. Don't spend days agonizing over it or being a martyr, just take responsibility and move forward.

Shifting your mindset from the day to day responsibilities of an individual contributor to the broader view of a manager and leader takes time and practice. Don't expect these skills to evolve overnight, and don't be discouraged if you have some setbacks as you try to strike a balance between getting things done and coaching/mentoring your team members. In the next chapter we will discuss time management, and delve further into the concepts of leveraging your time through the development of your team.

CHAPTER 6

Leveraging Your Time

In addition to shifting your focus with respect to your own accountability and the currency of leadership, you will be making another major mindset change as you transition into a management role. In your new position you will be held responsible for more work than you could possibly complete by yourself. This is a corollary to the earlier point about being responsible for the work of others. If you find that your team members are less efficient and/or less skilled than you are, you will be tempted to try to do the work yourself. As we discussed in the last chapter, this is a losing proposition for two reasons – first it is most likely impossible, and second it is counterproductive to your own success as a manager.

Instead what you will need to do is leverage your own time in a targeted and controlled fashion across the team to make sure tasks are completed in a timely matter at a high level of quality. Doing this while keeping track of your daily tasks and not losing sight of the larger goals of your team is a big challenge, and in order to achieve it you will need to implement some form of time management solution.

Time management is, at its most fundamental level, the division of larger initiatives into daily tasks, and the integration of those tasks into your daily work/life. While there are many systems available (See the Resources section for a list of organizations that offer training and complete time management solutions.), they all revolve around four key skills

> Breaking Large Goals Into Daily/Weekly Tasks
> Prioritization
> Task Management/Scheduling
> Delegation

In this section we will go over some practical strategies for developing these skills. If you are challenged by time management (if, for example you listed missing deadlines or losing track of tasks as a weakness in your personal SWOT analysis), I highly recommend that you invest in dedicated time management training from one of the vendors listed in the Resources section.

Building trust and developing strong relationships with your team, your colleagues and your customers are highly dependent on your ability to do what you say you will do, to meet deadlines, and to keep from forgetting important tasks. All of these goals are rooted in your ability to keep track of the things on your plate, and get them done in a timely manner.

BREAKING LARGE GOALS INTO SMALLER TASKS

How do you eat an elephant? You do it one bite at a time. You've probably heard this saying and many others like it before. In a management role, you won't just say it, you will live it. Goals that come down to you from upper management and objectives you set with your team will rarely be things you can accomplish in one day. There are entire books and training programs devoted to project management, and if that's a central part of your job, you will want to include that type of training in your personal development plan.

The first skill you will need to master is the ability to take a large initiative, sometimes presented simply as a metric or goal, and turn it into something that you can not only delegate to your team members, but track from a progress perspective. Let's use an example which we will revisit later on when we talk about setting goals.

Imagine for a moment that in your monthly management meeting, the CEO sets a goal to grow the organization by 20%. You are the manager of a team of outside sales representatives. So how would you go about taking that goal and turning it into an actionable plan for your team?

1. **Adapt The Goal To Your Team** – If the company wants to grow by 20%, then your team revenues will need to grow by 20% (it can be more

complicated than that, but for the purposes of this example we will keep it simple)

2. **List Activities That Contribute To The Goal** – These may be activities you already do such as scheduling sales meetings, or they may be new activities like purchasing a list of leads or sending out a mass mailing.

3. **Analyze the Inputs and Outputs** – If you currently complete 30 sales meetings per month, and close 10 deals out of those 30, you will need to figure out how many more meetings you need to have in order to close 12 deals/month (hint – it's not 2!). Take a look at your target and work backwards – you will find that you need to have 36 meetings if you continue at your current close rate of 33%

4. **Set Tasks** – Based on the example above, you now know that you need to generate at least 6 more meetings per month across your team. You can meet with your team members and brainstorm ways to increase your meeting generation numbers – do you need to make more phone calls? Launch an advertising campaign? Use this session to assign specific tasks to team members, and to make sure everyone understands the target, and buys in to the full plan to get there.

5. **Monitor Progress** – Once you have determined what each person on your team is responsible for in achieving this larger goal, you will need to add these items to your agenda for individual goals meetings, and create action items for yourself to follow up and ensure that progress is being made towards the goal.

There is more information on the specifics of goal setting and goal management in the Method section of this book, under Week 11. Once you have effectively divided a project into smaller tasks, you will need to assign a relative priority to that project and its associated action items, since it is likely that it will not be the only thing your team is working on at any given time.

PRIORITIZATION

Prioritization is the act of ranking projects and tasks according to their importance and level of urgency. There are always multiple factors that affect how you prioritize a task or a project. You might give higher priority to one item because a key customer asked for it or lower priority to another item because it doesn't directly tie to a larger goal or objective of your team.

One common way to prioritize tasks that you will come across in your management career is what's referred to as the "Eisenhower Method" or "Eisenhower Grid". Pioneered by President Dwight D. Eisenhower, this method suggests that you rank your priorities into quadrants based on where they fall on the scales of urgency and importance.

Table 3 - The Eisenhower Grid

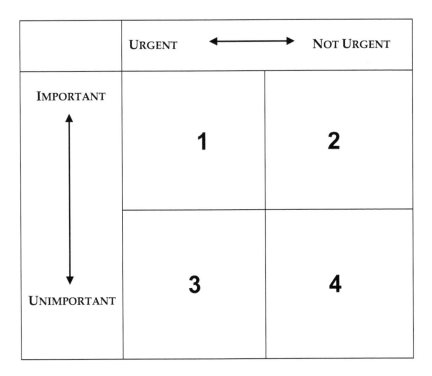

Anything in the top left quadrant (urgent and important) holds the highest priority. The top right and bottom left quadrants follow, and the bottom right quadrant contains items you should consider dropping off your to-do list.

Most people find that their major time management challenges are the tasks in the top right and bottom left quadrants. Items which are important but not urgent tend to get pushed aside for more urgent issues. As a result they don't receive the attention required until they suddenly become urgent (at which point it's usually too late to do them effectively).

Items which are urgent but not important are often the things that take up the time you should be spending on the less urgent but more critical tasks. A false sense of urgency creates high levels of unnecessary stress within your team, and tasks that fall into this quadrant should be considered for elimination.

This framework can be useful both in analyzing team goals and priorities, and helping individuals understand how to leverage their own time. If you have a team member who is struggling with getting things done, it can be helpful to have them lay out their priorities on this grid. You can then adjust some tasks, remove some priorities entirely, and make sure that you both agree on what falls into the urgent/important quadrant.

Once you have broken projects down into their component parts, and identified their priority rankings, you can move on to the processes of task management and scheduling.

Task Management/Scheduling

Making a list of things to do is usually the first step taken in the realm of time management. Having a visual representation of all of your tasks allows you to clearly see what's on your plate, and to decide when and how you are going to tackle each task. It can also be a source of motivation for you as you see progress through the number of items you complete and remove from your list.

Simply having a list of tasks is a great start, but in order to be efficient with your time, you need to categorize those tasks. As discussed in the previous section, one important classification is by priority. Putting your tasks in buckets according to how important and urgent they are will help you see what needs to be done first. The next step is to categorize tasks by the type of work involved.

Here's a sample task list for a Sales team leader:

Task	Due Date	Priority	Type
Goal meeting with Kate	Today	1	Meeting
Call Big Client, Inc.	Today	1	Phone Call
Send proposal to Little Client Co.	Friday	2	Task
Prepare agenda for Friday	Friday	1	Task
Call Small Vendor Corp.	Tuesday	3	Phone Call
Pick up dry cleaning	Today	3	Task

Even though the call to Small Vendor Corporation is not due until tomorrow and is a lower priority, this manager will probably choose to make that call today along with the call to Big Client, Inc. Why? Because he blocked off an hour on his calendar for phone calls, and he's planning to run through all of his calls at once while his team knows that he shouldn't be disturbed.

This leads into the calendaring and scheduling aspect of getting things done. Most businesses will use some type of standardized calendaring system, usually as part of their messaging and collaboration suite. Some use Microsoft Outlook, others use Lotus Notes, and smaller organizations may use Google Calendar or some other low cost solution. No matter what tool your company selects, you will want to make sure that you spend some time familiarizing yourself with how your calendaring system works.

Many electronic calendaring systems can connect to mobile devices such as smart phones. This allows you to keep your calendar and task list with you as you go to meetings and events, which can be very helpful if someone asks you about your availability. Your personal organizer can also remind you when you have tasks or meetings due. Make sure you pick up a book, or ask for training from your IT group (if your company has one) so that you can learn the best way to leverage the task and calendar management solution you are using.

Let's take an example of an IT team leader. She uses Microsoft Outlook to manage her tasks and her calendar. One of the things she likes to do is block off time on her calendar to work on specific initiatives. She can color code these blocks of time, which gives her a great visual picture of where her time resources are focused.

If she uses blue for internal initiatives, yellow for client support activities, and green for team management related tasks, she can take a high level look at each week/month and know what activities are taking up her time. It also allows her team and her manager to see what's on her plate, and find times within the appropriate blocks to meet with her about those specific areas.

This manager has also asked her team to use a specific color code for meetings and support activities that relate to the initiative of migrating users to the new email platform. She has created a calendar view for her whole team, and can easily see what percentage of their time they are spending on that activity without having to interrupt them for reports.

Scheduling blocks of time on your calendar to accomplish highly important goals is a good way to make sure that your time does not get used up on less important activities. Especially during the early phases of your career as a manager, you will want to identify your high priority projects and activities and allocate time to work on them. As you move through the 90 Day Action Plan in the Method section, block out time on your calendar for each of the action items you need to accomplish within a specific week. Using this method will allow you to be available for issues that come up in your group, but still maintain dedicated time to move forward on your longer term goals.

Learning how to organize, prioritize and schedule your tasks is a key skill for all employees regardless of whether or not they are in a management role or not. However the fourth aspect of time management (and the one that many new managers find difficult) is the process of dividing the work up among your team members. I am referring, of course, to the challenge of delegation.

DELEGATION

Delegation is a delicate art, especially when you are new to a management position. Many new managers tend to vacillate between micro-managing (i.e. breathing down the neck of their employees and poking them every time they need to do something) and being too far removed from the process (i.e. hiding in their office wondering what they are supposed to be doing.)

The goal of successful delegation is to isolate a specific task or goal, set a deadline and a definition of success, and then create a reasonable number of checkpoints along the way which will allow the task to be brought back on track if it has gone astray. Once that framework is in place, a task can be delegated in a sufficiently hands off manner that both you and your team member can keep track of it without undue stress. It then becomes the manager's job to keep track of the deadlines and checkpoints on an ongoing basis, freeing your team member to focus on the completion of the task itself.

The key to successful delegation lies in effectively defining the boundaries of the task or goal being delegated. Its achievement (or lack thereof) must be interpreted identically by both parties.

There are many solutions available to help you become more effective at time and priority management. The key to selecting an appropriate solution is understanding how you work and which option is most closely aligned with your needs. No system is a perfect fit for everyone, and you may need to try them in sequence until you find the one that works best for you.

CHAPTER 7

Thinking like a Business Owner

In this final chapter on mindset, I'd like to invite you to pretend that you own the company in which you work. Some of the best individual contributors and managers that I have ever met owe a large part of their success to their ability to think like business owners. In fact, while I am presenting this as part of a book about management, I strongly recommend that everyone should work towards this mindset.

A business owner understands every aspect of how his or her company makes money, and what attributes will lead the organization toward success. While they may not have the skills to perform every job, business owners take a high level view and understand that every job is necessary in order to achieve the goals of the whole organization. This is called systems thinking.

As a manager you will need to take a systems view of your team. A systems view means considering your team as a part of the whole organization and considering each member of the team as a part of that whole. As an individual contributor you may have had the luxury of focusing completely on your own work. As a manager you need to consider your team's work from the perspective of management, and your own management from the perspective of each team member.

What are some key components to thinking like an owner? The following are a few examples of ways in which you can shift your perspective from employee to owner:

> **Spend Like it's Your Money** – When you consider the monetary value of the tools and investments you want to make, think of them as if it were your money: the equity in your house or your own savings. In Chapter 13 we will discuss the skill of building a business case for spending, but you should always consider the cost from the perspective of what value it brings to the organization, and how it helps you achieve your goals.

> **Care About Your Work** – Many people will tell you that business is business and it's not personal. While that's true, it doesn't mean you should be approach it without any feelings at all. Caring about the quality of the work you do and the culture of your organization are key components of being effective as a manager. Enthusiastically

support team members when they do the right thing, and don't let things slide if they aren't good enough.

➢ **Strengthen the Brand** – No matter where you fit in the organizational structure, people will associate your work and your values with the values of the organization as a whole. Be a champion of your company's products and services, and be proud of the work that you and your team do.

➢ **Speak Up** – If you see something that isn't working right, let someone know. Whether it's your manager, Human Resources or the CEO, if you know something is preventing the company from growing or being its best, you can bet that the owner would want to know about it. You may be in a unique position to see the inefficiency of a process or the fact that a certain behavior on the part of management is eroding morale.

Thinking like an owner challenges you to consider different viewpoints on issues and will help you make better decisions and more thoroughly prepare for potential obstacles to your team's productivity. For example if you are implementing a policy change that affects how other departments interact with your team, you need to consider the impact of that change from the perspective of your team, your customers, your manage-ment and your vendors. Each constituency will have a different view of the change. Considering the impact from their perspective will help you build strong collaborative relationships for the future.

In addition to using systems thinking to evaluate your team from the outside, you should apply it to your team members as well. All managers should have a realistic understanding of the ebb and flow of their team's lives outside of work. That is not to say that you need to be best friends with your direct reports, or that you need to delve into your team's personal lives. It's more that you should make an effort to understand that an individual's performance and motivation is not static and varies according to what else is going on in their world outside of work. As such an individual might be highly productive and motivated for several months, and then become distracted, burnt out or otherwise unmotivated due to something happening in his or her life outside of the office.

It is important that you, as a new manager, make an effort to be attuned to the variations in your team's motivations. Rather than punish the person for their drop in productivity, it's better to try to find the root cause and offer some flexibility. If you proactively approach an employee whose work seems to be dropping in quality or quantity, and offer to adjust their workload accordingly for a few months, you will find that they turn out to be even more motivated and productive in the future. Using a pro-active, flexible approach will build both trust and loyalty with your team, and encourage them to work hard when they need to, but to maintain a healthy balance. This will avoid your being blindsided by an employee suddenly quitting or dropping the ball in a major way.

In the best case scenario, you will build an environment where your team gives you realistic information about their ability to perform at their peak. Then when you really need them to come up with a little extra, they will be happy to do so.

MINDSET WRAP-UP

Adapting your mindset to your new role can take time. If you have been working as an individual contributor for many years, your automatic response will be the mindset of a team worker, not a team leader. The only way to transition is through daily practice. As a starting point I recommend that you put yourself on an active reading plan using the Resources section of this book. Reading a chapter or two every night will bring fresh ideas and new energy into your daily work.

You can also post some visual reminders around your office to help keep your new priorities in the forefront of your mind. Find a motivational quote to use as your desktop wallpaper or a poster to hang on your wall. Join a network of managers in your field, and find a coach or a mentor with whom you meet on a monthly basis. These activities will help you maintain your focus through some of the tough days. Before long these new habits will become second nature.

PART 3

METHOD

CHAPTER 8

The 90 Day Action Plan

Month 1 – Get to Know Your Team

T he first 90 days of your new management role are critical to your success. That's not to say you can never change course again, or that if you are past the first 90 days, you have nothing to worry about. If you feel that you have been ineffective as a manager and want a fresh start, you can implement this plan at any time. However if you are just starting a new job, it's the ideal way to get off on the right foot. When you follow the steps outlined in this plan you will:

- Develop a complete picture of your team

- Understand your organization's goals and targets as they relate to your team
- See how you are viewed by your customers both internally and externally

The objectives are not designed to fill up your entire week. My assumption is that you will be responding to requests, working on tactical issues and communicating with your team and your supervisor throughout this period. Rather these goals are designed to provide you with a framework of the key tasks you will need to complete in order to ramp up into your new position. While there is logic to the order of the weekly tasks, you can re-arrange them if you need to or if a need arises to complete a step before the scheduled timeframe.

As you move through the 12 week program, you will be practicing the systems thinking skills that were introduced in Chapter 7. Viewing your team and yourself through the lenses of your team, your customers, your vendors and your manager will help you identify personal and group strengths and weaknesses, and then develop plans to deal with challenges before they become crises.

The 90 day plan is divided into three sections, one for each of your first three months. In this first month you will focus on getting to know your team, its individual members, and how you contribute to the larger success of the organization. As you move through these months, try not to rush the process. The tendency of many new managers is to jump in and make major changes on the first day. This can lead to trouble if you are acting without knowing all of the facts. Take your time to build relationships with people, and to truly hear what they want and need from you. Doing so you will greatly improve your chances of success in the longer term.

WEEK 1

Get the Facts about Your Team

Action Items

- Request Personnel Files for Team Members
- Identify Impending Deliverables
- Request Team Budget
- Request Compliance Information

Objectives

Your first week in any new job will no doubt include a number of conversations with the Human Resources Department as you complete your initial paperwork. This is a great time to request information on the current performance and qualifications of the members of your team. Ask to review the personnel file for every employee that you will be responsible for managing. This should include the following information for each employee:

- Salary and title history
- Performance reviews and goals
- Resume and qualifications
- Disciplinary activity or other issues

This information will provide you with a baseline when you schedule your more detailed meetings with team members in week 3. You will need to be familiar with each person's strengths, weaknesses, communication style and goals in order to be an effective team leader. As we discussed in Chapter 3, a key aspect of motivating your employees is allocating work according to the level at which it challenges the person doing it. Ideally you want to have each team member feel that their work is neither boring nor overwhelming. The key to achieving that goal is having a thorough understanding of their skills and competencies.

In addition to obtaining information from Human Resources about your individual team members, you should schedule a quick meeting with your staff to introduce yourself and actively seek out any impending deliverables. Let them know that you will schedule a full review of all projects shortly, and meet one on one with everyone over the next few weeks, but that if anyone has key deadlines or deliverables that need immediate attention, they should let you know right away. There is nothing worse than being blindsided by a deadline of which you were unaware. Make sure you query your direct supervisor for this information, as well as your team members.

Your first week will probably include some interaction with the Finance Department as well as HR. If it does not, make a point of sending an email to the Director of Finance or whoever is in charge of the budget for your department. You may be able to get this from your direct supervisor, depending on the size of the organization. While some of your budget may be out of your control (if it applies to your department as a whole and you are a team leader, for example), it is worthwhile understanding how you fit into the cost structure of the organization.

Finally, if you are working for a publically traded company, an environment that processes credit cards, or if your company must comply with any of the myriad compliance standards that apply to many industries, you should request information about what compliance goals apply to you and your team. It may be as simple as completing change management forms, or as complex as reporting on multiple KPIs (Key Performance Indicators). Whatever the situation, you will want to familiarize yourself with what's required of you and your team, and make sure your operations are in line with the organizations compliance needs from day one.

WEEK 2

Take Stock of Current Projects

Action Items

- Meet with Team to Review Projects
- Identify Deliverable Risks
- Create Visual Timeline

Objectives

Kick off your second week by scheduling a meeting with your team to have a full review of all open projects and deliverables. Ask your team to come prepared with a list of the projects on which they are working, including the following information:

- Customer (internal or external) to whom the project relates
- Milestones and timelines for completion
- Dependencies from other departments
- Obstacles (if any) to the successful completion of the project

To make it easy, ask each member of your team to code their deliverables or projects as green, yellow or red depending on their confidence that they will meet their deadlines. This may result in you having to turn your attention to getting some projects back on track, or communicating a change in timeline to a customer, but it's far better to be proactive about this issue in the early weeks than to let it derail you further down the line.

Ideally you will walk away from this meeting with a better grasp of your team's workload. If you were promoted from within this team you may be familiar with the projects on the table, but it's unlikely that you had all of the details of each project. Assuming you know where things stand without verifying your facts is risky – it's far better to approach your team's work as if it were entirely new to you than to gloss over the details and potentially miss an important point.

If you identify any projects with deliverables that are at risk of not being met, don't try to delve into them in this meeting. Make a note of the basic information (project name and specific team members involved) and schedule a separate meeting to discuss these issues. You can then establish a plan to resolve the issues and get things back on track with the team members who are involved without taking up the time of all of your staff.

Once you have a complete picture of the projects on your radar screen, make a visual (ideally on a whiteboard so you can update it as things change) representation of your team's workload in your office so you can see at a glance how things stand. Then if you are asked for an update on the status of any initiative, it will be at your fingertips. You should be the only one that makes changes to this board – if your team can walk in and erase/reposition deliverables you will quickly lose control of your change management. You can create a process where the project leader notifies you on a daily or weekly basis of any changes so you can update the board.

Depending on your specific organization or industry, you may have more or less project related work in comparison to the on-demand work your department produces. If you are in a heavily project oriented environment, you will want to ensure that your personal project management skills are a strength. The Project Management Institute provides a training and certification program which can be highly valuable for individuals who have strong need for project management skills as part of their daily job function. More information on this organization is available in the Resources section.

WEEK 3

Get to Know Your Team Members

Action Items

- Schedule Individual Meetings
- Compare Meeting Results with Team Facts

Objectives

In Week 1 you gathered data about your team from the perspective of the organization by reviewing personnel files and qualifications. After completing that exercise you should have a basic understanding of each individual's qualifications, their history with the company, and how they have been performing to date. This week your goal is to uncover how each person on your team views their goals, their personal strengths and weaknesses, and their contribution to the team as a whole.

Be prepared to spend most of your time listening during these individual meetings. This is not a time for you to tell people what you want them to do, it's a time for you to hear directly from your team members how they feel about their work, what challenges they have, and what goals they are trying to achieve. To get this information you will need to engage in active listening, which is a key management skill.

Active listening has four core components:

- Listen to what's being said
- Observe the body language and demeanor of the speaker
- Rephrase and repeat to ensure you understand
- Ask clarifying questions

Start off the conversation by asking each team member to describe a typical day and to list some of their priorities and goals. Listen carefully, not just to what they say about their daily activities, but how they look. Do they roll their eyes? Are they talkative and willing to share information or do you have to drag each piece of information out with a question?

You will definitely want to take notes during these sessions, but spend as little time as possible writing. Jot quick notes and reminders, but spend most of your time looking at and interacting with your team members. If you hear a statement that you don't understand or that is not clear, ask clarifying questions to draw out the details. Make sure you truly understand what's being said by rephrasing what you hear and repeating it back to the person with whom you are meeting.

Later (in Week 11) you will circle back to your team and have a second set of goals meetings. In those sessions you can collaboratively adjust and update goals with each person in your group. For this meeting however, you are simply trying to get a picture of how each individual feels about their job, what goals they have, and what challenges they face.

Take the information you gather from these meetings and compare it to the data you received from Human Resources in Week 1. Look specifically for discrepancies or things that don't seem to add up. For example a team member who gets excellent performance reviews and seems well qualified for their position might appear unfocussed or disinterested in your individual meeting. These types of observations will help you spot potential issues and draw them out before they become larger problems.

Your goal, where feasible, is to make sure that the work you have assigned to your people is challenging enough to keep them motivated and happy, but not so challenging that they feel overwhelmed or unable to be successful. Having a good handle on the capabilities of your staff will help you achieve this balance. With this information in hand you can go back to the Employee Motivation Matrix in Chapter 3 and do an initial categorization based on your impressions from these meetings.

Keep in mind that your observations represent a point in time in your team members' day. If you catch someone on a bad day, they may come across as unhappy and unfocussed when in fact they are actually quite satisfied with their situation. Any time you observe negative behavior or perceive that someone is unhappy with their working environment, take a note of it but continue to observe their actions over the next week or more before you bring it to their attention or try to create a plan to resolve the issue.

WEEK 4

Understand the Metrics of your Department

Action Items

- Obtain Metrics Used to Evaluate Your Team
- Request Meeting to Establish Expectations of Upper Management
- Request your department budget

Objectives

In Week 1 you had your first meeting with the finance department, and ideally obtained some basic information about your group's budget. This week you will be delving into the details of how your department is measured, and what you need to be aware of to be successful.

It can be a big eye-opener to view your department through the lens of the Finance Department. Before you reached the management level, you probably believed that your goal was to produce the best product possible, provide the best service possible, or make as many widgets as you could in a day. What you may not have realized is how much analysis goes into the management of daily operations even in relatively small organizations.

Let's use an example of a common business management metric. Most organizations that have customers and sell products keep track of a metric called "churn".

Churn represents the change in the number of customers who are buying the company's product across a specific period of time. Sometimes this is a positive number (existing customers buy more stuff or increase their service plans) but often it's a negative number (existing customers cancel their service or choose not to buy anything).

Churn is often used to measure customer satisfaction, and companies often set a threshold of acceptable churn. The idea is that the Sales Department will bring in a certain amount of new business every month which will offset any loss of business to competitors or downturns in sales volume from existing customers. As long as there are more new sales than there is churn, the company will grow and make money.

So as a manager, if you run a customer service group, you may be held accountable for minimizing the amount of negative churn. You might be given a target number (what's known as a metric or a KPI) and you will need to work with your team to ensure a sufficient rate of satisfied customers or resolved issues which in turn minimizes the monthly churn.

There are many ways that companies measure their performance. Understanding which metrics apply to you and your group, and then developing strategies to impact those metrics in a positive way are key functions of a manager.

One of the most commonly understood and utilized metrics is the budget. A budget in the business world follows the same concepts as a personal budget, but can be more complex. It is essentially an estimate of spending by the group on items such as salary, equipment, tools and supplies. Spending within a business structure has to be approved by the management team (with the input of the Finance Department) to make sure that the company as a whole does not spend more than it earns.

Each department is generally required to submit a budget to the Finance Department on a recurring basis. Usually the budget is created or approved at the end of one fiscal year, and applies to the next fiscal year. You may think that a year is from January to December, but in many organizations the fiscal year does not line up with the calendar year.

Discovering the budget cycle for your organization is a key goal for this week. If you are hired in September, and the budget cycle follows the fiscal year, you will need to work with your manager to estimate what costs will be associated with your department in the coming year. This will include salaries, tools, training, and equipment for your group to accomplish its goals.

If you are moving into an existing position, it's likely that a budget will already exist, in which case you will want to review it and see what the projections look like, whether you have any money left to spend, and when the next budget is due. If you are in a newly created department, you will want to schedule a meeting with your direct supervisor and/or someone from finance to create a new budget.

You may be surprised to learn that a budget already exists based on historic spending patterns. Accountants and finance folks like to fit spending into their projections, and will often create information for you if you (or your predecessor) haven't created it yourself. While this might provide you with a jumping off point, it most likely will not include money for new initiatives, training, or tools you might need to make your department more effective.

Having a solid understanding of the budget and other metrics of your department will help you align your goals and the goals of your team with the goals of the company as a whole. You should actively seek out and build relationships with the finance team as they can be strong allies in helping you uncover what upper management wants from you, and how you can provide the information they need to report on the performance of your group.

CHAPTER 9

The 90 Day Action Plan

Month 2 – Customers and Vendors

Once you have established a working relationship with your team, and have familiarized yourself with the projects and deliverables for which you will be responsible, it's time to proceed to the next phase – getting to know your customers and vendors. The majority of managers are viewed as the face and voice of the team to both external and internal customers and to vendors. It is important that you represent the needs of the team, and are the conduit for inbound and outbound requests.

Customers and vendors are two sides of the same coin. You provide goods or services to your customers, and obtain the same from your vendors. Given that fact, it only makes sense to treat your vendors with the same level of respect and fairness that you hope to receive from your customers. While you may be nodding and saying "how obvious", I am always surprised at how many managers feel that vendor management involves posturing and browbeating rather than open communication and compromise. A high quality relationship with a vendor can mean that you get preferential treatment when you are under the gun, so that you don't have to shout and stomp your feet to get what you need. In the next few weeks we will walk through the process of building these relationships, and understanding the mechanics of setting expectations with customers and suppliers.

WEEK 5

Identify Key Customers and Stakeholders

Action Items

- Identify External Customers
- Identify Internal Customers

Objectives

Regardless of your industry, department or specific role, you have customers. They may be true external customers – for example if you manage a customer service department at a software company, your customers will be the folks that purchased your company's products. If you are a purely internal department such as IT or Human Resources, your primary customers are the other departments within the organization to whom you provide services.

Even if you fall into the second category, it is wise to know something about your company's external customers. Whether or not you service them directly, it's likely that your company culture is related to the people or companies who purchase your goods and services. A key component of being an effective manager is whole systems thinking. This means that you not only focus on the day to day processes of managing your department, but you are also aware of the larger goals of the organization and how the departments within the organization work together to achieve those goals.

Your objective in discovering the identity of your external customers and how they bring revenue to the organization is to understand how your team adds value to the organization as a whole in obtaining, servicing and retaining those customers. Irrespective of your own performance and the output of your team, your organization's ability to satisfy its customers is fundamental to its continued existence.

When learning about your internal customers you are seeking to understand how your department relates to the other parts of the organization. A web of interdependence exists within all organizations. The Sales team cannot sell without the Marketing Department. There would be no one to do the selling or marketing without Human Resources. No one would have the tools to do their jobs without IT, and no one would get paid without Finance.

You don't have to study advanced business theories and build relationship diagrams to get to know how your organization works. Your goal is to understand which groups need things from you, how they go about requesting those things, and how you go about requesting things from other parts of the organization. There is etiquette involved in departmental relations, and it's easy to get off on the wrong foot with someone else in the organization by ignoring or disrespecting their processes. Let me give you a quick example of what I mean.

You are standing on the pitcher's mound playing baseball with some friends. There are two people on base; your team is covering their positions, and a member of the opposing team steps up to the plate. Suddenly someone comes onto the field with a soccer ball and starts kicking it around. How would you feel about this new person's behavior? You don't want to be a source of frustration to other parts of your organization by showing disrespect for the established rules of the game or barging in without finding out what's going on first.

As a new manager you are walking into a game with rules, processes and established methods of communication. If you fail to take the time to get to know those rules in advance, you will have a long uphill battle to regain the trust and respect of your fellow managers.

Next week you will schedule meetings and actually spend time getting to know some of the other department leaders with whom you will be working closely, but the goal for this week is to uncover and understand who they are, and what processes they have already published (usually in operations manuals or on an intranet). This information will allow you to start your conversations on a respectful and positive note because you have already familiarized yourself with what exists. Once you get going you may discover that some managers are willing to bend their own rules. Initially, however, you should make sure you know of and abide by their published rules.

WEEK 6

Meet your Customers and Stakeholders

Action Items

- Schedule Meetings with External Customers
- Schedule Meetings with Internal Customers

Objectives

Last week you reviewed the history of your external and internal customers. This week, armed with that information you can move into a phase of outreach and start building relationships with these individuals. Depending on the total number of customers you serve, it may not be possible to complete all of the meetings in one week. Your goal is to reach out and begin the process of getting meetings on your calendar that will take place over a period of a month or more.

So what are you going to talk about in these meetings? Your goals here are almost identical to the goals you had in Week 3 when you sat down with each member of your team. You are seeking information about how each client perceives their relationship with your organization as a whole and your group in particular. To obtain that information you will use the same active listening and observing skills that you practiced with your staff.

Here are some specific agenda items for your meetings with external customers:

1. **Review Outstanding Deliverables** – Compare what you learned in Week 5 with what the customer is expecting – are you on the same page or do you need to adjust expectations?

2. **Request Feedback** – You have an opportunity to start your relationship fresh with each customer. Find out what their experience has been in the past, what worked well, and what they would like to see change.

3. **Schedule Follow Up** – Depending on the client type and how you typically interact with clients and customers, you will want to establish a communication pattern. Sometimes you will be calling them on a weekly basis. Other times you might meet them in person once or twice/year. Establish a baseline for how your customers preferred mode of communication – do they want email updates, phone calls or scheduled face to face meetings?

This is an instance where you will want to take careful notes and (if you are in a truly customer facing department) enter this information into some sort of central location so that everyone on your team has access to it. This can be as simple as saving a document on a central file server under a folder with the clients' names, or as complex as using a fully integrated CRM (Customer Relationship Management) system.

No matter how you accomplish it, you will want to make sure that you keep track of the information for future reference, since your customers will not feel that you value them if you ignore the information they have given you.

Last week you also identified the departments with whom your group works most closely. Your department will have indirect interaction with almost every other part of the organization. It's possible to make a case that everyone in the organization is, in some way, an internal customer. For practical purposes, however, and certainly for the duration of your first 90 days, your time should be focused on those groups with whom you interact most frequently, and particularly the departments that depend on your group in order to function.

If you are brought on board as the manager of a sales team, your first job will be to develop strong relationships with marketing, customer service, finance and manufacturing. Depending on your industry this might be development or professional services, whichever group actually produces the product that you sell.

In the last section I recommended that you read the operations manual (if one exists) for each department with whom your group interacts. Ideally each segment of the organization will publish guidelines and timeframes on how they provide service to other parts of the company. If these don't exist, your goal in your meetings with the other department leaders is to document this information for yourself and your team. Let's take a specific example.

Let's assume that you have been hired to manage a team of recruiters. Every department relies on your team to post job advertisements to the company web site, as well as to career boards and other external resources. Submitting a job posting to your group involves following a defined process of obtaining approval for the job requisition, specifying the salary, skills required and reporting structure, and handing the information off to your team along with the text of the job posting. Provided this information is submitted correctly, you can give the other departments an accurate estimate of when the position will be posted, and what you will do with résumés as you receive them.

All of this information should be stated in a document which you can provide to other groups to help them understand how to use your services efficiently. These documents provide the foundation for inter-departmental relationships, and can help avoid misunderstandings.

If your group doesn't have a documented operations manual, or any other way of communicating what other departments can expect from you and your team, you should develop one. These guideline set clear expect-ations of how your group operates under normal circumstances. You can always bend the rules for exceptions, but having the standard process documented is more efficient as you can simply refer people to it when they have questions.

Building strong, productive relationships with other departments can be highly beneficial to your success as a manager. If you are known as someone who communicates clearly, keeps your word, and is respectful of the processes of others, you will have many advocates to help you through the challenges you encounter.

WEEK 7

Gather Vendor Information

Action Items

- Obtain (or Create) Vendor List
- Determine Whether Vendors Can Be Changed

Objectives

Over the next two weeks you will be continuing the process of getting to know key individuals and organizations that interact with your team, understanding their perspectives, and building strong relationships with them. This week we will be talking about vendors – the companies (and individuals) who provide services and supplies to your department.

Let's start by talking a little bit about who and what vendors are, and why it's worthwhile to build strong vendor relationships. These organizations (also known as suppliers) provide goods or services to your company as a whole or to your department specifically. Why should you bother getting to know them? For the same reason that you work to develop strong relationships with your customers – a mutually beneficial vendor relationship adds value to both organizations and can be a powerful tool to help you accomplish your goals.

Vendor relationships are identical to customer relationships, except that in this case you are the customer. What makes a good vendor relationship? A mutually beneficial scenario comes from a good match between the services that a vendor supplies, and the needs of your organization or group. You receive products and services that you need to do business, and your vendor receives revenue in return.

What could go wrong with that process? Several things can contribute to a vendor relationship becoming less than productive from either the vendor's perspective or yours. Here are just a few possibilities:

> **Changed Product Offerings** – Most suppliers evolve their product offerings over time. Sometimes that evolution means that what you have been purchasing is no longer available or no longer considered a primary or profitable product to the vendor. In this case you may see the quality of the product you receive degrade because your vendor is no longer focusing on it. Ideally, your point of contact with the vendor will communicate this type of change to you, but in some circumstances you will not receive this information directly and will have to seek it out yourself.

> **Price Increases** – Over time, most vendors will increase their prices. In fact it's common practice to raise prices on existing customers while offering discounts to attract new business. This can mean that you are not getting the best value for your money by being unwaveringly loyal to a

vendor when their own prices or their competitor's may be lower if you chose to switch.

➤ **Staff Changes** –Your relationship with a vendor will be closely related to your relationship with the account management and sales professionals that handle your business. If there are staff changes on the vendor side you may experience a loss of continuity in your service. Previous arrangements may be forgotten (deliberately or accidentally) and you will have to work to build up a new relationship with the supplier as if you had just begun doing business with them.

➤ **Mergers and Acquisitions** – At times a vendor will go through a transition such as being bought out or merged with another company. This can have the combined effect of changed product offerings, price increases and staff changes.

➤ **Process or Capacity Issues** – Suppliers sometimes encounter a period of growth which exceeds their capacity or the ability of their internal processes to deal with the number of orders or clients they have at that time. If you see a drop in responsiveness or time delays in receiving products, it may be due to an overload of orders on the supplier side. This can be a temporary condition or a more sustained problem, depending on how the vendor adapts to the change in business.

You should review your relationships with your vendors on a regular basis to ensure that the arrangement continues to be beneficial for both your own organization and the supplier. You may not have complete control over whether you continue to use a specific source, but you can collect and provide feedback on the performance of the vendor to other managers within the organization, and have input into whether that organization continues to be used.

As a first step in the process, you will need to identify the vendors with whom your department or team interacts on a regular basis. Here are some examples of vendors – these can vary widely depending on your industry and function within the organization:

- ➤ Office Supplies
- ➤ Hardware (Laptops, Machine Parts, etc.)
- ➤ Software
- ➤ Consultants
- ➤ Printers
- ➤ PR/Marketing Services

Gather your vendor data into a single location so you can organize the contact process. Here's a sample worksheet you can use to collect data about your vendors:

Table 4 - Vendor Evaluation Template

Vendor Name	Product	Authority to Change?	Contract End Date	Feedback

As in Week 1, your task this week is to gather as much information as possible about who the vendors are, how they have performed in the past, what type of relationship the organization has with them and whether there is a contract in place requiring you to work with them for a specific period of time.

Once you have identified your vendors you can move on to reaching out on an individual basis and building relationships with your points of contact. Most vendors will welcome the opportunity to review your account with you, and help you get up to speed on how their products and services work. Naturally they will present themselves as being the very best at what they do, and you will need to do your own research to confirm or deny those facts. Initially your goal is simply to know who to go to for various services, and identify any vendors that you might want to change in the future.

WEEK 8

Contact Vendors

Action Items

- Reach Out to Vendors to Notify Them of a New Point of Contact
- Request Proposals to Compare Prices

Objectives

Last week you identified the key suppliers for your group. Now it's time to start the process of reaching out to these vendors and determining whether you want to continue working with them, or whether you want to consider making a change. Divide your vendors into two groups – those you can't change but need to get to know, and those who are up for review.

For organizations in the first category, your goal is simply to make contact with them and let them know that you are the new point of contact for your department. If you already have copies of existing contracts and pricing, and things are going to continue as they have been, your conversations can be short. Some vendors may want to come in and meet you in person while others may just want to have a brief phone call. It's worthwhile to note how you feel about the treatment you receive from your vendors, as it's likely that your own customers will be making similar observations. If you see something that a vendor does which makes you feel truly valuable as a customer, consider integrating it into your own routines with your customers.

For vendors and suppliers in the second category, your goal is to let them know that you are reviewing their status with your organization, and would appreciate reviewing their contracts, seeing their best pricing, and possibly meeting with them to more fully understand their offerings.

Always treat your vendors the way you would want your customers to treat you – be fair and honest in your evaluation and communication. If you are unhappy with the service you receive, let your account representative know, as you may be able to get the issue resolved and continue the relationship. Most organizations are highly motivated to retain customers and to keep them happy.

There are a couple of key terms and processes that you will encounter when you are working with vendors. Larger organizations require you to obtain bids from competitors in order to decide who will provide service to the organization. Depending on the scale of your company, this may be a formal process or an informal one. It's always a good idea to compare prices; however you may not always choose to go with the lowest bidder (unless you are required to by company policy). So how do you obtain competitive bids?

In an informal organization you might just find three companies in the phone book or on the internet that offer the service or product you seek. You can call them up, request a quote, and then make your choice based on that. For small purchases that will usually be the way to go.

For larger organizations, big projects, or government agencies, this process is structured and includes the development of an RFP (Request for Proposal). This document is used to define all of the aspects you expect to see when a vendor bids on a project. By clearly articulating the variables, you can (ideally) easily compare the proposals you receive in an "apples to apples" way.

There are many templates available on the internet to help you develop an RFP but at its basic level any RFP should include the following elements:

> **Company Overview** – What does your company do and how will this project, product or service contribute to your company's success?

> **Description of the Need** – What exactly are you looking for and what does the proposal need to include in order to be considered?

> **Response Format** – How do you want vendors to reply? Can they send the proposal electronically or do you require a hard copy? To whom should they direct their proposal?

> **Timeframe and Follow Up** – Over what period of time will you be soliciting bids? Will vendors receive a response regardless of whether or not they are selected?

You may see this process referred to as RFQ (Request for Quote) or RFI (Request for Information) but they generally refer to the same process.

CHAPTER 10

The 90 Day Action Plan

Month 3 – Vision and Goal Planning

Over the last two months you have gotten to know the key individuals with whom you will be working on a daily basis. You have started the process of reaching out to these stakeholders and getting your relationship off on the right foot. While this work is important and must continue for you to be successful in your new role, it's time to spend some time looking up from your desk and into the future.

Management often involves keeping your eyes focused on two event horizons simultaneously. You will need to be aware of the daily processes and activities of your team while also planning and preparing to achieve the longer term goals of your department. This can be a bit of a juggling act in the first few months, and I strongly recommend that you allocate half a day, at least once per week, to work on your strategy and to plan for these larger initiatives. It's easy for them to get lost in the shuffle as you put out fires on a daily basis, but if they get permanently lost you will be not be effective in your new role.

Over the next three weeks we will review the mechanics of goal planning; from creating a vision which will help guide the activities of your team towards the larger organizational goals, to developing individual blueprints for each team member which will facilitate their own development. The most important thing to keep in mind with goal planning, as with delegation, is that you are ultimately responsible for the outcomes of your team. You can (and should) delegate authority, which gives your team members the ability to pursue initiatives on your behalf and on behalf of the team. You can also hold your team members accountable for their performance with respect to these goals, but ultimately the responsibility for getting the team to perform their duties and achieve their goals will always rest with you.

To be an effective leader and manager you need to feel personally responsible for the output of your team, without tipping over into being a micro-manager or doing all of the work yourself. In the next three chapters you will learn the tools you need to maintain that balance effectively.

In the final section we will go over how to prepare for your first review with your own manager. Taking all of the data you have assembled over the last few months, you will be ready to report on the state of your team, request any resources to prepare for the coming month, and hear feedback on your own performance to keep you on course.

WEEK 9

Build a Team Vision

Action Items

- Meet with Your Team
- Brainstorm Team Goals and Attributes of Team Success
- Bring Challenges and Obstacles to the Surface

Objectives

A vision statement is a great way to clearly articulate the overarching goals of your team. Many times during the course of your daily work you will need to make judgment calls about the priority of various issues. A vision statement can act like a compass to help you decide what things are most important to help you achieve your goals. It's easy to get lost in the details if you don't have a destination in mind. Here's a quick example.

The Newport to Bermuda race is an annual event where yachtsmen and women come from all over the world to compete in a 3 day ocean race between Newport, Rhode Island and Hamilton, Bermuda. The main strategic obstacle in this race is the Gulf Stream – a broad, warm water ocean current which flows northward along the Atlantic coast. My father participated in this competition with team of experienced navigators aboard a yacht belonging to veteran sailor and expert navigator George Clowes.

Over the course of 3 days and nights, the team members sailed and navigated the boat in shifts, usually 4 hours on and 4 hours off. On the first night of the race, three of the crew members, including my father, were hunched over a chart debating the relative merits of taking a tack offshore. They were comparing the weather reports which said that the wind was better further to the east, and the Gulf Stream chart which showed a particular area where the current would be more strongly against them in that area.

As they carried out their discussion, George came up on deck. He listened to both sides for a few minutes and then asked the team a key question. "Which way is Bermuda?" They gave him a compass heading and he responded "Sail towards Bermuda" and went back down below to finish his rest. While the "straight up the middle" approach is not always the appropriate solution, you cannot be successful if you don't know where you are trying to get to in the first place.

Developing a vision statement for your team helps you in creating alignment between your team's individual goals, the larger department goals and the organization as a whole. This short statement (usually 1-2 sentences) encapsulates the value that your group brings to the larger organization. It acts as a lens through which you can view the activities of your team to determine whether they are in line with the ultimate goals you are trying to achieve.

To build a vision statement you first need to brainstorm a list of words and phrases that describe aspects of success for your group. Some examples might be:

- Most referred
- Most accurate project estimates
- Highest in customer satisfaction
- Always on time
- High quality work

Use these phrases to build a sentence that includes several aspects of how your team's success is measured. For example a customer service team's vision might be:

"We strive to exceed our customers' expectations by solving their issues through accurate information gathering, efficient service and thorough follow up."

Your team's vision statement should reflect the relationship between your group and the rest of the organization, with specific reference to how your team adds value and contributes to the overall company goals. For example if your company has a goal of growing by 30% in the next fiscal year, and your team is part of the sales group, you might develop a vision that looks like this:

"To facilitate the growth of The Amazing Company by 30% through indentifying, proposing and closing 30 new deals each month."

Once your team has developed a vision statement, make it visible. If this phrase or mantra encapsulates the goals of your group, it will help keep it at the front of everyone's minds if it's prominently displayed around the office. Revisit the vision statement on a regular basis to make sure it remains relevant, and revise it if needed to ensure that it represents the key components of success for you and your department.

WEEK 10

Set Long Term Team Goals

Action Items

- Review Company Metrics and Objectives
- Meet with Manager to Define Departmental and Organizational Goals
- Identify Large Scale Initiatives Related to Goals
- Identify Individual Activities Contributing to Goals

Objectives

Over the last 9 weeks you have had conversations with many of the stakeholders whose needs you must meet. At this point you should be prepared to consolidate all of those needs into goals and projects, and to work with your team on outlining a timeline in which the activities will be completed.

Ideally, each goal or target that you set should roll up into larger department or company objectives so you can build alignment into every aspect of the work of your team members and the broader needs of the organization.

Alignment is a hot topic in management. You may have heard it batted around in meetings and if you have been through a restructuring recently, it was probably cited as one of the reasons behind the re-org. But what's all the fuss about? What is alignment and what does it mean to you and your team?

Most organizations have goals and targets at many levels. At the top are revenue and profit related goals, and as these filter down through the organization they become sales targets, churn metrics or other KPIs (Key Performance Indicators) which show up on your job description or in your department meetings as initiatives. In an ideal world, every task or initiative being actively worked by any member of the staff should roll up to some larger organizational goal. This is the true definition of alignment – the act of lining up your goals and processes such that they all point towards the same larger objectives.

In practice business communication is rarely this effective. Top down management can often feel like a game of telephone – the senior executives get together for an offsite and build a strategy. These plans are brought to the directors of each department who are in turn responsible for making them into action plans for their teams. As the goals are diluted, restated, interpreted and otherwise passed around, they become less and less clear until finally someone tells the receptionist that she needs to start wearing a red wig and clown shoes.

So how do you figure out how to keep your team's goals tied to the big picture of your company's success?

- **Get In The Loop** – Ask to see the memos, documents or other primary sources of information when new goals come down from above. Don't rely on what's said in meetings (or worse what you remember later if you didn't take notes); try to get the data from as close to the originating sources as possible.

- **Compare Existing Goals** – Anytime a new goal appears on the horizon, you should take the opportunity to lay them alongside your existing initiatives. Does the new goal conflict or work at cross purposes to anything that you are currently pursuing? If so you will need to bring that up the food chain and figure out which goals stay and which goals go. Bringing up this type of anomaly can help clarify situations where targets have been improperly communicated as they came down from the top.

- **Use Common Sense** – If something doesn't make sense, don't just follow the lemmings over the cliff. It is a rare (and unsuccessful) business management team that deliberately implements goals that have a negative impact on the organization. With that said there are times when upper management is not fully aware of the impact a change may have on internal processes. So don't just wear the clown shoes and wig without double checking.

Alignment is a powerful tool to help businesses achieve their goals – having all of the individual contributors moving in the same direction avoids inefficiencies and improves morale. However without effective communication it's easy for the message to get lost or confused on its way down through the layers of personnel. Your job as a team leader is to be sure you are finding ways for your team to be marching in the parade, not driving the clown car. Here are some more activities and approaches to long term goal management.

1. **Identify Initiatives Which Are Not In Alignment**
    If you uncover a project which does not tie back in some meaningful way to a larger company or customer objective, highlight it and determine whether it should be eliminated.

2. **Identify Initiatives Which Fail to Meet Goals**
    You may find projects which, while they are aligned with larger goals, are failing to meet the targets they were implemented to achieve. Highlight them and determine whether they need to be adjusted or cancelled and replaced.

3. **Prioritize Issues on the Important/Urgent Scale**
    Revisit the Eisenhower Grid in Chapter 5 and evaluate each project on that basis. If you discover that a particular initiative falls in the unimportant/not urgent quadrant, consider it for elimination.

By evaluating each project on the merits of alignment, probability of success, and importance/urgency, you can refine the goals for your group and potentially eliminate some unnecessary work. This will make room for new initiatives which are more closely tied to the needs of your customers and the targets of the organization as a whole.

This process will usually require three phases – first you will review the goals yourself, then you will review them with your team to see if there is any information about them of which you were unaware, and finally, you will review them with your direct supervisor to ensure that there is no issue with cancelling particular items.

WEEK 11

Create Individual Goal Plans

Action Items

- Schedule Goals Meetings with Team Members
- Review Existing Goals in Context of Team Vision and Organizational Goals
- Lay Out Short, Medium and Long Term Goals
- Identify Required Tools and Training

Objectives

At this point you should have all the information you need to sit down and review, adjust, and refine the goals of your team. You have uncovered the requirements of all of the constituencies that you need to satisfy, including your internal and external customers, upper management and the growth needs of your team members. To complete the process you will be sitting down for 45 minutes to an hour with each person on your team.

At the end of this process you will have reviewed everyone's goals and made sure you understand them, and that they are aligned with and support the objectives of your team and the company as a whole. Then schedule quarterly (or even monthly) meetings with each member of your team to review, prioritize, and get updates on the status of their progress towards these objectives.

HOW TO SET GOALS

As we discussed earlier, a major aspect of your new management job involves the effective setting and monitoring of your team's goals. This process is a collaboration between you, your manager (and the stated goals of your organization as a whole) and your team (both individually and collectively).

It's easy to come up with ideas for goals, keeping in mind that your goals should have certain characteristics which allow you to make sure that they are achieved in the way that you would like. One of the most common goal definition methodologies currently in use is the SMART acronym. A SMART goal has the following characteristics:

- **S**pecific
- **M**easurable
- **A**ttainable/Achievable
- **R**elevant
- **T**imely

Let's go through each attribute and see some examples of how you can use this in practice.

Specific

A specific goal is one that is clearly defined. If you have an employee who has been slacking off in submitting their time sheets, you could set a goal that says "be more prompt in submitting your timesheets."

However that would not meet the criteria. Instead you should say "submit all timesheets by Friday at 4PM over the next 12 weeks". The second phrasing clearly articulates exactly what you want the individual to do in order to be successful.

Larger goals should also be specific in nature. For example, if your sales target is to grow new sales revenue by 20% over the year, rather than saying "everyone should sell more", you would want to attach some metrics to the goal. This can involve some complex calculations, but it ultimately results in a goal that your team members understand clearly and can work towards on a daily basis. So to grow new sales by 20%, you might have to analyze what your close rate is currently and then set a number of meetings or sales presentations per month that would increase your total number of sales by that amount. Here's an example of how to do the math:

Current Close Rate = 33% (that means that for every 3 meetings with customers you close one deal)

Current Monthly Sales = $100,000/month

Average Revenue/Sale = $1000 (that means that on average, each deal you close is worth $1000)

Number of Team Members = 10

Increasing sales by 20% means you want the current monthly sales number to move to $120,000/month. To do that you will need to have about 60 more meetings per month ($20,000 = 60 x .33 x $1000) than you currently have. If you are still with me after all the math, you can now divide 60 meetings across your team members and give them a specific goal of scheduling and delivering 6 more meetings each in order to achieve the target. That's a much more specific goal than "schedule more meetings" or "get more revenue".

Measurable

A measurable goal is one that has a defined output that you can count. Both of the goals in the example above are measurable. You can count how many times your employee turns his time card in on-time and you can count how many meetings per month each individual schedules. This allows both you and your team member to clearly understand what is being expected of them.

Sometimes you will need a tool in order to measure the output of a goal. For example if you are a manager in a Human Resources Department, you may have goals that relate to employee satisfaction or positive feelings about job performance. To capture the data on whether or not this goal has been achieved, you will need to send out a survey. When you are setting goals that require feedback from employees or customers, you should always survey them twice.

First, you will need a baseline to find out how they respond to the situation prior to your enacting any change. Then, you can set a goal for your team to change a process or implement a new program, let it run for a period of time and then survey your customers again. If you don't measure the baseline status before you implement the change, you will not be able to see whether or not you have achieved your goal.

Attainable/Achievable

Almost everyone is familiar with the scenario of a manager entering the conference room and announcing a goal for the team that is completely impossible to achieve. There is nothing more likely to reduce morale or frustrate your team than to put out a goal that can't be reached. While you should challenge your team, the challenge should be based in reality, not fiction. Using the example of the sales goal above, it would be possible for a manager to decide that his team should not just achieve the goal but vastly overshoot it.

While the theory of over achieving can be a positive one, if it puts the goal out of reach and strains the capacity of the team beyond a reasonable level, it's a bad idea. The mark of a good manager is one who is aware of what's on the plate of each team member, and who can figure out a goal which pushes the team members to do their best without burning them out. It can be healthy to set two levels for larger goals – a realistic goal and a stretch goal.

The stretch goal represents a scenario where you (and upper management) will not just be satisfied with the result, but will feel that the team gave a little bit extra. Ideally, you will have some leeway to reward your team for this sort of achievement. Whether it's giving them a half day off, an unexpected bonus (a gift card, for example), or some sort of recognition within the organization, there should always be a tangible benefit for going above and beyond what was asked.

Relevant

Don't create goals just for the sake of having them. If your team feels that you are creating work just for the sake of having something for them to do, they will rapidly lose respect for you. Similarly, you should avoid creating artificial deadlines. It is better to set the correct deadline and follow through with consequences if a team member fails to meet the timeline than to create a situation where you continuously extend the finish line.

Both of the sample goals above meet the relevant test. Time sheets are a necessary administrative process and if you permit your employees to turn them in late, you are inconveniencing another department. By doing so you are creating tension and bad feelings between your department and Human Resources. This goal is relevant because it maintains a positive relationship between your team and another internal department.

The second goal is relevant because it ties directly to a larger goal of the organization. This helps to build alignment, where everyone in the organization is working towards the same destination, and is therefore willing to help and support one another.

Timely

A timely goal is one with a clearly defined end date, which is a key component of effective time management. In Chapter 6 we discussed how to break large goals down into daily and weekly tasks, and how to apply those tasks to a calendaring system. By agreeing at the beginning how long it will take for a goal to be completed, both you and your team members will be able to plan appropriately for its completion.

When you are considering the timeframe of a specific goal, it's important not to be arbitrary about it. Ideally, you should have a rough estimate of how long it takes to complete a task. If it is a long term process which involves variables that are out of your direct control, you will still need to apply time boundaries. These can come in the form of checkpoints or milestones that are reviewed on a scheduled basis (weekly or monthly). You can also apply time limits to pieces and parts of the goal, but leave the more variable areas open and agree to narrow down the timeframe when you have more information.

Goal setting and goal alignment are key themes in effective management. If I could choose the most important piece of advice in this book, it would be the information in this section. Work with your team to develop SMART goals that are aligned with the objectives of the organization, and you will be well on your way to being an effective manager.

WEEK 12

Review Your First 90 Days

Action Items

- Create a Team Status Report
- Schedule a Meeting with Your Manager
- Request Feedback on Your Performance
- Share Feedback and Needs of Your Team

Objectives

Congratulations! You've made it to the finish line and now it's time to take stock of your first 3 months and prepare to build on the lessons learned during this critical first period. As you mentor and coach your own team and have regular goals meetings to keep track of their targets, you should institute the same structure with your manager. Ideally, your manager is on the same page with you regarding the importance of setting and aligning goals throughout the organization, in which case you can work together to keep information flowing from the top down. If not you will need to actively request information regarding the expectations and needs of upper management.

To prepare for this meeting you need to pull together all of the information you have gathered over the last 90 days and be ready to talk about the challenges as well as the successes of your team's performance. For each of the following areas, prepare a brief summary (a paragraph or so is plenty) describing the key points for each group:

- **Team** – List any issues or concerns you uncovered in the first few weeks, and describe how you are addressing them. If you have completed your team vision, state it here and describe how it reflects the goals of your group. Put a timetable of your short and long term team goals into this section as well.

- **Customers** – Discuss your progress in meeting with your internal and external customers. If you have uncovered any concerns or have changes in the way you interact with your clients, list them here. Comment on your relationships with internal customers, including the outcome of any meetings with other department managers.

- **Vendors** – Describe your status with the suppliers your team utilizes and whether you intend to put any projects out for bid using the RFP process. If there are vendors you cannot change, relate any information or feedback you have obtained in this section so it can be passed on to the appropriate people within the organization.

- **Budget and Metrics** – Outline your team's progress towards achieving the metrics you uncovered in Week 4. If you have concerns about your budget, or have purchases you would like to make, include them in this section so you can have a discussion about their value to the team.

While this meeting will likely be informal (it's not a performance review), being prepared will help you make the most of your managers time and will set the tone for future meetings. By doing your homework and making sure that you have the facts at your fingertips, you will show that you have not been idle over your first few months, and that you are making strong progress towards being an effective manager.

Once you have put together your key team facts into a written report, send the information to your boss in advance. This will provide her or him the opportunity for to review the data points and develop questions or comments. When you are in the meeting itself, you can clarify specific points and ask for feedback related to your progress.

No matter how thoroughly you prepare for this meeting, or how well you have done over the last 12 weeks in integrating yourself into the culture of the organization, it's likely that your manager will have some feedback and suggestions of ways in which you can improve. If you were a rock star as an individual contributor, you may be accustomed to receiving glowing performance reviews with little or no areas for improvement. However, as a new manager, you can and should expect to have new growth areas and aspects of your performance that need improvement.

Be open to constructive criticism and feedback. Hopefully, it will be offered in a positive manner but even if it's difficult to hear, this is the information you need to help you grow and become more successful in your new role. It's also likely that your manager and your organization will have specific items on which they want you to focus that are beyond the topics in this book. While the 90 day success plan is a great general guide to getting yourself up to speed as a new manager, success within your specific industry or organization will go beyond what we discuss here. You should actively seek out resources from your manager and your network of industry contacts to use as you build your personal development plan.

Feedback is a two way street. In addition to receiving an evaluation of your own performance and providing information about the progress of your team members, this is your opportunity to ask for tools and resources, and to provide information about your experience as a new manager within the organization. Make sure you read Chapter 14 – Creating a Personal Development Plan prior to this meeting. If you have identified any training courses or other activities which you feel would enhance your performance, bring them to your manager's attention. You may not be able to get approval for everything on your list, but you should definitely take advantage of the opportunity if there are items that your company is willing to pay for or support you in doing. Most managers will be happy to see you take initiative for your own development and will support your efforts in this area.

90 Day Action Plan Wrap-Up

The first 3 months of your new job may be some of the most challenging of your career. Transitioning to a supervisory role will push you to grow as an individual, develop new skills, and harness your own personal strengths in ways you may have never considered possible. Completing this period is just the beginning.

Continuing your journey in management involves building on the lessons you have learned in your early days and committing to improving your skills on an ongoing basis. In this section we covered some of the many tasks and objectives involved in getting to know your team, your colleagues, your customers and your vendors. As we move into the final two parts of this program, you will learn how to measure and track your own success and that of your team, and how to build momentum to move forward in your career.

PART 4

MEASUREMENT

CHAPTER 11

Evaluating Your Team's Progress

W e have talked extensively over the course of this book about setting, aligning and tracking progress towards goals. But how do you evaluate whether or not you are making traction towards your objectives? How do you know when you have "made it"? There will be many different components of how you and your team are measured, and each of the various groups we have discussed (your team, your manager, your customers and your colleagues) will value different things about the work you produce and your management style.

In this chapter we will talk about some specific ways that you can evaluate your team's progress and performance as a whole, which is probably the way you will be measured by your own manager. We will focus primarily on objective metrics that you can track and monitor over time. In addition, we will discuss how you can build an effective communication process with your own manager which will help you keep on top of how you are being perceived.

There are three major ways of measuring a business system. You can quantify inputs, processes and outputs. Input metrics involve activities or behaviors that you have asked of your team which are designed to generate an output, but do not by themselves accomplish the full goal. When we talked about the sales team which was working towards growing by 20%, their input was the number of meetings scheduled. The goal was to move the output (the number of new contracts signed) by simply increasing the number of meetings with customers and leaving other processes and procedures in place.

Another approach they could have taken would be to focus on the process. By changing the pitch they were using, or adjusting the potential customer screening process, they could have increased their close rate to 40% which would have accomplished the same result in a different way.

The most common business metrics are output related. You've probably heard the term "results oriented" in job postings and job descriptions. This statement implies that you will be judged on your outputs. You may focus on the output numbers when you are reporting on the progress of your team, but you cannot change the results without looking at the inputs and the processes that affect them.

Figure 2 – Aspects of Measurement

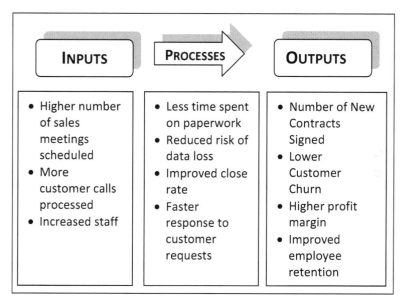

One of the challenges in measuring anything is having the data in the first place. Some things are simple to measure: you can count the number of new clients that sign contracts in a given month or the number of new employees hired within a given period of time. Other things are more difficult to quantify. How do you measure customer satisfaction, for example?

You could look at your churn numbers and assume that all of the customers that leave your organization do so because they are dissatisfied with your service. However, that may be misleading – it's possible that you are actually losing customers because your competition is selling the same product for a lower price. You could send out a survey or request feedback, but you might only hear from your happy customers and be under the false impression that everything is great.

Many managers (and even some companies) fall into the trap of trying to measure everything. They have so many metrics that they spend more time counting things than they spend on building customer relationships or selling products.

The goal in effectively evaluating your team's performance is closely tied to your original task of building a team vision. If you have boiled down the key value that your group brings to the company as a whole into just a few short sentences, they probably include the metrics you should focus on. Let's revisit the two sample vision statements we talked about in Week 7.

> "We strive to exceed our customers'
> expectations by solving their issues through
> accurate information gathering, efficient
> service and thorough follow up."

In this example, the manager would be best served by creating a customer survey with the sample survey on the following page.

Figure 3 – Sample Customer Service Survey

Customer Service Survey

1. Did your experience with our customer service department...
   a. Exceed your expectations
   b. Meet your expectations
   c. Fail to Meet your expectations
2. Did you feel that your customer support representative thoroughly and accurately understood your problem?
   a. Yes
   b. No
3. Was your customer support representative sensitive to your time?
   a. Yes
   b. No
4. Did you receive a follow up call to ensure that your problem was resolved correctly and completely?
   a. Yes
   b. No
5. Was your issue resolved correctly and completely?
   a. Yes
   b. No
6. Is there any way your experience could have been improved?

This simple survey could be administered to a random sample of customers, and could be sent out anonymously to provide the most accurate feedback. If you track this feedback over time, you would see whether your group is delivering service according to the vision of the department, or whether a change is needed. The second sample vision is even clearer:

> "To facilitate the growth of The Amazing Company by 30% through indentifying, pitching and closing 30 new deals each month."

The target is straightforward – company growth of 30% and a team target of 30 new closed deals per month. In both cases the "what" question is answered within the vision statement itself, leaving it up to you and your team to develop a plan of how to hit those numbers.

A well crafted vision can help you focus on the key metrics that you and your team feel are necessary in delivering what you see as your department's true value proposition. You may also have metrics assigned to you from your manager and upper management.

CHAPTER 12

Conducting Performance Reviews

A college friend of mine once said she wanted to write a diet book. On the first page she would write "eat less", and on the second page she would write "exercise more". I was tempted to use that as a template for this chapter since the fundamentals of performance reviews are just that simple.

> ➤ Praise the Good
> ➤ Correct the Bad
> ➤ No Surprises

If you have succeeded in developing goal plans with your team members, and have been meeting quarterly or monthly with them, a performance review should be nothing more than an extended goals meeting. You will probably be required to complete a form as specified by your Human Resources department, (and ideally, this will not be the first time that either you or your team member has seen that form) but otherwise your aim is to go through your team member's performance in a structured manner and provide feedback and correction where appropriate.

PREPARING FOR THE REVIEW - EMPLOYEE

In preparation for a performance evaluation, you should ask the individual you will be reviewing to complete a self evaluation. I usually use the actual performance review template for this so I can compare the employees' rating of themselves with my rating of them and identify any areas where we diverge. I recommend sending the self evaluation out a week or so before the actual review will take place, and asking the person to return it to you 24 hours prior to their review. You can also simply ask them to bring it to the review. The goal here is not to line up your answers with theirs, but to create a talking point during the review itself based on how they view themselves vs. how you perceive their performance.

In addition to preparing a self-evaluation, you should ask your team members to bring a status report on their major goals and initiatives. You should already have this information from recent goals meetings and project updates, but having a completely up to date version can be helpful in evaluating progress and identifying any targets you may want to change or re-prioritize.

PREPARING FOR THE REVIEW - MANAGER

As you approach an employee evaluation, you will need to gather some specific pieces of information about the performance of your team member in order to provide an accurate assessment of their performance. At a minimum you should obtain the following:

➢ **Salary and Bonus History** – Many performance evaluations include the opportunity for salary increases or bonus payouts. Be sure to get a complete history of the employee's previous increases and bonuses. If your Human Resources Department has the data, compare each employee's salary to industry averages for their title so you know how competitive their salary structure is. If you can't get this information from Human Resources you can use online tools such as www.salary.com to get an estimate.

➢ **Feedback from Customers** – If your team operates in a customer facing capacity, you may have information about this employee's performance from evaluation forms or direct contact from the client.

➤ **Feedback from Colleagues** – If you receive information from team members or other individuals from inside of the organization over the course of the review period, file it so you can easily access it at review time.

➤ **Achievement of Goals** – From your goals meetings with your team members, you should have a documented record of their performance including completed goals, outstanding objectives, and general performance.

One technique for performance reviews has gained popularity over the past few years. This evaluation method, called a 360° review, includes feedback from peers, managers, customers and direct reports. While there are many formats and templates for a 360° review, it's basically just a form you send out to individuals with whom your team member interacts, requesting feedback on specific areas of their performance. It can be helpful to solicit this type of information from other constituencies in the organization so that you can get a more thorough picture of how the individual is perceived from different perspectives than your own.

Whether or not you are using the 360° review format, prior to the review you will need to complete a form rating the performance of the individual over a stated period of time. While individual performance evaluation forms vary widely by organization, they commonly include some of the following elements:

1. **Employee Title and Salary** – This section shows what the employee earns currently. Occasionally this includes a check box or field for you to indicate if the employee is eligible for promotion.

2. **Performance Ratings** – In this section you will likely be rating individuals on a scale of 1-5 (sometimes more or less, but 1-5 is very common) with 1 being unacceptable, 3 being average and 5 being outstanding.

3. **Narrative** – After the structured performance ratings you will usually have an area where you can comment broadly on the performance of the individual, discuss their progress towards their goals, and lay out a growth path. To reduce the possibility of employee lawsuits, some organizations use software applications to generate this text from the performance ratings or from pre-written statements.

Before completing any review form, make sure you sit down with a representative from the Human Resources Department and/or your manager and review the implications of ratings and reviews on salary increases and bonuses. If reviews were simply about feedback, people would be less concerned about them. The reality is that most performance evaluations tie directly back to raises and bonuses, and as such, employees will pay strict attention to your ratings of their performance.

Based on the three components of an effective performance review I cited above, your first priority is to praise the good. Identify areas where this individual excels, and if possible use specific examples of great work. I keep a folder for each employee in my e-mail filing system, and anytime I appreciate a contribution of theirs, or receive an e-mail from a colleague, customer or team member which identifies good work, I file it in their employee folder. At review time I can pull up all of the feedback, both positive and negative, and use specific examples in my evaluations.

After you have identified the great work, it's time to offer constructive feedback and criticism. In the cases of both positive and negative feedback, the performance evaluation should not be the first time the team member has heard about these issues. Open communication about strengths and growth areas is a key component of effective employee development. You should be sharing feedback with your team and the individuals on it whenever you receive that information. However, in the privacy of the performance evaluation you can review in detail any areas where your team members need to improve, and set goals or brainstorm processes by which those improvements can be made.

Documentation of positive and negative feedback, progress towards goals, and the impact of tools and resources to enhance performance is a critical component of management. At times you will encounter an employee who, despite your efforts to work with him or her, will fail to meet the expectations of their position. In these instances you not only need to provide consistent, frequent feedback in an effort to improve the situation, but you also need to keep a record of your communication with them in case they ultimately need to be terminated.

Your Human Resources Department or company management should provide you with the tools and resources you need to complete performance evaluations. Be sure that you take the time to understand what is expected of you as a manager in terms of these reviews, and that you are thoroughly familiar with the process, as this is surely something on which you will be evaluated in your own review!

CHAPTER 13

Creating a Personal Development Plan

If you've come this far, you have probably noticed something about me. I am not Peter Drucker, John C. Maxwell, Dale Carnegie or Stephen Covey. While I admire their work, and try to incorporate the ideas of great leaders and managers into my own practice, I never, ever try to be anyone other than myself. One of the first steps in being an effective manager or leader is to be authentic. You cannot pretend to be someone or something you aren't, no matter what you perceive the rewards to be.

In the very first chapter we talked about the tasks and skills of a manager because if you don't truly enjoy doing those things, there's no point in reading any further. It is not worth a dump truck full of money to spend your days doing something that frustrates you or puts you in the position of doing things you strongly dislike. There will certainly be days where you feel challenged and even uncomfortable in your new role, but at a basic level you should be trying to build on your own skills, not shoehorning yourself into someone else's personality.

The good news is that if you have read all the way to this point, you probably do enjoy the challenges of management, at least enough to read a book on the subject. Assuming that you want to carry on, let's talk about how to create a personal development plan for yourself that will help you work through the highs and lows of your new career.

In the first chapter you completed the exercise of creating a personal SWOT analysis. If you didn't do it then, take the time to do it now. Uncovering what you bring to the table and clearly identifying areas where you need development are the keys to both your growth and ultimate success in your career. Your goal in creating this plan is to build on your strengths (not ignore them) and mitigate your weaknesses.

Your SWOT analysis is a good representation of your current state. It shows you where you are today and what you bring to the job. The next step is to develop a representation of where you want to be in the future. First, lay out the items from your SWOT on a grid (see Table 4 on the following page).

Table 5 - Personal Development Exercise

Item	SWOT	Goal	Reason
Enter items from your SWOT analysis on these lines	Enter the SWOT Category	Describe where you would like to be with this item in future	Put in your motivation for wanting to achieve this goal
Example 1: I'm a great public speaker	Strength	I want to incorporate more speaking events into my career	Being able to articulate my position on things in a public forum will help people perceive me as a leader
Example 2: I forget to follow up with people	Weakness	I want to be known as someone who always get back to people	It erodes my relationships with my customers, colleagues and my team when I don't follow up with people

You may notice as you move through this exercise that there are some goals which are related. For example attending a time management course might help you achieve multiple goals. Place these goals together so that in the next exercise you can treat them as a group.

Once you have identified a goal for each entry on your personal SWOT analysis, prioritize them based on the Eisenhower Grid we discussed in Chapter 6. Rank importance based on how much this skill relates to your success as a manager. For example getting a handle on your time management skills is both important and urgent. Developing your public speaking skills is important but not particularly urgent. Remember that personal development is a long term process so it's fine if you have a lot of items on your list as long as you don't try to do them all at once!

For each group of goals, identify specific actions that you can take to build the skills you need to achieve your objective. This is the most research-intensive part of the process. Here are some ways to find out what tools and tasks can help you achieve your goals:

> **Talk to People** – Seek out people who have the skills you seek and ask them how they got them. Did they read books? Attend seminars? What do they recommend for you?

> **Search the Web** – Spend an hour or two on the internet and search for the skills you want to build. Look for common themes or programs that lots of people seem to recommend.

> **Ask Human Resources** – The Human Resources Department often keeps a library of training materials, books, and articles which can help you develop specific skills.

Once you have narrowed your options down to a few target programs or resources for each goal, you can turn them into tasks to incorporate into your daily life. To transition these goals into actionable items you can move onto your calendar and to-do list, you will need to identify a timeline for completing each initiative. Here's a sample grid to help you lay out goals on a quarterly basis

Table 6 - Goal Planning Template

Goal	Q1	Q2	Q3	Q4
Improve Time Management Skills	Read The 7 Habits of Highly Effective People		Attend Time Management Seminar	
Increase Personal Network	Create profile on LinkedIn	Join Networking Group		Attend Networking Event
Complete Technical Certification	Course #1	Course #2	Sit for Exam	

While you may have the best of intentions for creating a plan and sticking with it, sometimes you will have to re-arrange your initiatives due to competing priorities. There's nothing wrong with being flexible, and I recommend that you stretch your personal development process out over time so that you don't get burned out from trying to do too much at once.

An ideal personal development plan is a source of personal motivation. You will be able to see your progress towards these goals which will help you be successful not only in your current environment but in every aspect of your career. Companies value individuals who seek to improve themselves. You may find that your organization wants to be an active partner in the funding and management of your personal development plan. Ask about tuition reimbursement before you pay for things yourself, and see what tools and resources are available to you as part of your employment benefits.

Measurement Wrap Up

Developing yourself and your team is an iterative process. You gather data through the measurement process, implement a plan (usually expressed in terms of goals and targets), and them measure the effect of that plan to see how far you have come. Then you make adjustments to your plan and go back to gathering data again. Without measurement and metrics, businesses and individuals would have no idea whether they are making progress. Your ability to develop methods to measure your team's inputs, processes and outputs will allow you to see how you are doing from an outsider's perspective.

It's easy to get caught up in the numbers and to spend so much time measuring and evaluating that you forget to act. Remember that measurement is only one of the five aspects of effective management we have discussed in this book. While the metrics are important, they should not be your only focus.

Also keep in mind that the numbers you are watching may vary widely over short periods of time. Avoid the temptation to adjust course for every fluctuation. When you are driving towards something to your south, the road is rarely straight, but you don't worry about the small curves because you have a map and know that ultimately your course will get you to your destination. Use numbers as a check to make sure you are on track, but don't veer from guardrail to guardrail with every bump in the road.

PART 5

MOMENTUM

CHAPTER 14

Hiring Great People

U nless your position involves creating a new department, the majority of your team members will probably come with the job. However, sooner or later as a manager you will need to bring a new team member on board. Your first goal will be to hire people who are a good fit for both the responsibilities of the job you are seeking to fill, and for the culture of your team. Make sure you evaluate each candidate based on the Employee Motivation Matrix from the Chapter 3. Your goal is to find candidates who fall into the can/will quadrant.

Depending on the size of your organization, your Human Resources Department may provide you with guidelines, assist you in recruiting, and even pre-screen some or all of your candidates. If you need to hire a new staff member, your very first trip should be to the Human Resources group to understand their process and see what they need and expect from you.

DEVELOPING A JOB DESCRIPTION

In all likelihood, the first thing you will need to produce is a description for the position you are seeking to fill. If you are filling a position due to turnover, or adding a staff member to an existing type of position or role, you will simply need to find (and possibly revise) the existing information. If no description exists, you will need to create one.

Every person on your team should have a job description which describes their position responsibilities and metrics for success. Your Human Resources Department may have a template that they require you to use, or you may be able to design your own. On the following page is a sample which you can use to get the idea of the components needed in a good job description. Keep in mind that this document and the metrics for success that it includes will form the foundation of the goals you set for this individual and all others with the same title in your group. Metrics for success should adhere to the SMART goal setting criteria described in Week 11 of the 90 day success plan.

Figure 4 - Sample Job Description

Job Description - Editorial Assistant

The Editorial Assistant performs administrative duties in support of the day-to-day operations of the Editorial Department. As directed by the Editorial Director, the Editorial Assistant has responsibilities in the following areas:

1. Responds to incoming calls and routes them to the appropriate staff member
2. Responds to requests for information about submissions with appropriate forms and information
3. Requests ISBN numbers for new books
4. Requests advance monies for authors according to their contracts
5. Acts as a liaison between the Production Department and the author as books move through the production process
6. Maintains contact information for all current authors

Metrics for Success:

- External customers receive responses within a reasonable timeframe (according to the timeframe matrix)
- Production department receives accurate and timely information about books in the pipeline and any changes to the schedule or status of those books
- ISBNs are received by the deadlines requested by the Production Department
- Authors receive advances and other monies according to the terms of their contract.

Once you have created a job description and you clearly understand where this individual will fit in the context of your team as a whole, you can start the process of screening potential candidates for the position.

FINDING CANDIDATES

Remember the help wanted ads in the newspaper? Recruiting used to mean writing up an advertisement and posting it either in print or on some type of job board. Today these methods are still used, but the majority of candidates come from posting the job on the internet or through referrals. Print ads were costly, so recruiters would write short paragraphs about their target candidate and expect to sift through huge volumes of résumés to find the right person.

Internet job boards and postings on company web sites allow you to provide a far more thorough description of the position, working environment, ideal qualifications, and other key points. Further, your job description is not just a posting of what you want, it's an advertisement designed to attract a highly qualified person. Your goal is to make this posting compelling to the right people so you get to choose from the best candidates. So how do you do that? Here are some tips for developing a great job posting:

> **Working Environment** – Create a list of key benefits your organization offers. Are the working hours flexible? Do you have a great location? Has your company been selected as one of the best places to work in your industry or area? To get

the best applicants you want to highlight the best features your company has to offer.

➤ **Compensation and Benefits** – These days base salary is only one of the components of employee compensation. A great benefits package, retirement programs, extra vacation time and bonuses are all things that attract high caliber candidates.

➤ **Opportunity** – Back in the Motivation section we talked about the five factors on which individuals judge their job satisfaction. Opportunities for career growth, learning new things, and advancing in their careers are important to highly motivated individuals. Be sure to list what opportunities are available within the organization and from a career perspective that make this job attractive.

➤ **Skills and Credentials** – Be specific about the experience, certifications, and other factors required for this position. While some candidates will apply even when they don't possess the skills or credentials you list, you want to rule out as many unqualified people as possible. That being said, be realistic about what you are asking for. If it's a must-have, by all means list it, but if you don't absolutely need it, make sure you specify it as preferred so you don't turn away potentially great candidates.

> ➢ **Specifics** – Make sure you cover the location, general working hours and preferred application process in your job description. If your job requires a car, if you are open to local candidates only, or if you have a specific deadline for applications, clearly state these items in your posting.

One of the best ways to find out if a job posting is compelling is to run it by your team. If you are adding a person with similar skills to the team members you have in place currently, they can tell you whether the listing is attractive, and what factors would make them apply for the position if they saw it.

Many managers try to pretend that their employees don't surf the job boards to see what else is out there. It's totally unrealistic to think that your team members never look at the market. Your goal is to build a great culture and environment that motivates them to stick with you and your organization. You can do that most effectively by accepting the fact that people will look around and by fostering open communication among your team members so that you will find out if someone is considering going elsewhere.

After you have developed a winning job posting, it's time to circulate it and see what you get for responses. Your Human Resources Department will post it to major job boards and media outlets. Your job is to circulate the posting to your personal network, and seek out referrals. Many great candidates come from "warm" leads – they are referred to you by people you know or by friends of friends. Professional social networking tools such as

LinkedIn and Spoke can help you keep track of your business contacts, and pass along job postings and other information. A lead from a personal source can often be the best way of finding a suitable candidate who is already working elsewhere.

Depending on the industry and how competitive the job market is at any given time, you may want or need to work with a recruiter to find candidates. A recruiter is a professional individual or organization that specializes in sourcing candidates for a particular field. Some are fairly general and have candidates across multiple industries and job titles, while others operate in a specific niche such as portfolio managers or environmental engineers. Recruiters generally charge a fee to the hiring organization that is based on the salary of the position you are seeking to fill.

Often, when you post a job you will be contacted by recruiters to see if you are interested in their services. Be sure to communicate with your manager and Human Resources department before you talk to a recruiter about the position. Many recruiters use high pressure sales techniques and will send you candidate information before you have an agreement in place to use their services. Unless you have a recruiting budget for this position that includes a fee for outside contractors, you will need to work with traditional posting and network outlets first. If you cannot find a candidate that meets your needs and you believe that a recruiter can help you, you can present it to your manager as a business case. Be sure you have obtained detailed information on the cost of using the recruiting service, their refund schedule if the employee doesn't work out, and exactly how their service works.

CONDUCTING INTERVIEWS

Once you have identified some potential candidates for your position, either through reviewing their résumés, a personal recommendation from a friend or colleague, or an internal application from a team member or other company employee, you will move on to the interview process.

Selecting someone to become a member of your team is a decision that should not be made casually. Keep in mind that you will be interacting with this individual on a daily basis, and their skills, personality and motivation level will impact every other member of your team. Because of this you should not be the only person who interviews potential candidates. Make sure that you have at least one other team member present during the interview, and when you narrow your candidate pool down to the final 2-5 individuals, have each of them come in and meet the whole team.

Prior to meeting with an individual, meet with your team members and lay out their roles in the interview process. Each team member should be responsible for evaluating the candidate from a specific angle. For example, you can have your most skilled technical team member evaluate them on their skills, including quizzing them on specific knowledge required to be successful in the position. Involving other team members in the interview process helps you achieve several goals:

➤ **Observation** – At a minimum, having another member of your team in the room will allow you to observe the candidates reactions to questions, their communication style and overall manner.

➤ **Varying the Process** – Sitting in a room with one person answering questions can be a tedious exercise. By interacting with different individuals and being asked a variety of questions, the candidate will be more engaged in the process and you can get a better sense of how they respond to different personalities and situations.

➤ **Team Buy In** – If you have built a solid team culture, you will want to make sure that the majority of your team members feel that this person will fit in well with the group. It's not necessary for everyone to love them, but if you get the feeling that most of your team members don't support this candidate, you will have difficulty assimilating them into your environment.

The interview process allows you to see beyond a list of credentials and understand some of the intangibles such as motivation, attitude and interpersonal skills that are not visible on their resume. There are many resources available on the topic of interview questions and techniques. I have listed some of them in the Resources section, and your Human Resources Department can provide you with further information on this subject.

MAKING AN OFFER

Once you have identified the person you believe is a great fit for your team, you will need to make them an offer of employment. This is another area where you will collaborate closely with the Human Resources Department. Most companies have a standard offer letter format which includes key information such as salary, benefits, start date and title. However before you send out an offer letter you will probably make a call to offer the candidate the position and find out if they are willing to accept the terms you have in mind.

The impression you make when you offer a candidate a position on your team can be a deciding factor in whether or not the candidate accepts the position. This conversation is a starting point for the tone of your relationship. There are some key points to cover during this call in order to close the deal with your ideal new employee.

1. **Be Enthusiastic** – While the process of interviewing and considering candidates can be long and arduous for you, it's equally grueling for the candidate. While they may be excited to come on board, changing jobs is a big and risky decision for most people. Your job is to help them feel that they are making a great choice. Make sure you let them know that you are excited about them and that you value their skills and experience.

2. **Be Specific** – Have a cheat sheet on your desk when you make this phone call with bullet points

including the specifics of the job. Go through each one in order and make sure you ask the candidate if they understand or whether they need more information about a specific topic. Miscommunication about salary, benefits or working hours can have a serious negative impact on your working relationship – make sure you are both on the same page about the position facts.

3. **Get an Answer** – Your goal with this call is to offer the position to the candidate and get their acceptance. It's common for job seekers to ask for some time to review the terms of the offer, or to give you an answer after discussing it with their family. While these are reasonable and acceptable, you want to have a clear understanding of when they will respond to you, and what information they need from you in order to make their final decision.

4. **Be Supportive** – In many cases an applicant will go to their current employer and give their notice. At that point a round of negotiations will ensue where their current company attempts to keep them from leaving. You can't prevent this from happening, so make sure you keep your second and third choice candidates in the pipeline while this process takes place. Keep your lines of communication open with your number one choice. Ask them to let you know if their company counter-offers, and what (if anything) you can do to encourage them to make the

change. Since this can be an anxious time for both
of you, enlist the support of your manager, the
Human Resources Department, and anyone else
within the organization that can help you make
the case that this position is the best choice for
your candidate.

5. **Be Prepared** – Despite your best efforts, your first
   choice of candidates may turn you down. Until
   you have an acceptance signature on the offer
   letter, don't tell the other candidates that they are
   out of the running. If you need to go to your
   second or third choice, you will want to approach
   them with the same level of enthusiasm as if they
   were your first choice or you will run the risk of
   losing them as well.

6. **Be Patient** – Finding the right person to join your
   team can be a time consuming process. You may
   be tempted to settle for a candidate that's only so-
   so, or to hire someone even though you don't feel
   strongly that they have the skills or motivation to
   do the job. Rather than give in to that temptation,
   keep looking until you find someone who really
   fits well. The process for terminating an employee
   who is a bad fit and the impact on your team as a
   whole will be far more painful than waiting a few
   more days or weeks for the right person.

After you have completed the extensive and complex
process of bringing a new team member on board, you
have one more task to complete before you can move

them back to the individual motivation topic and start building a goal plan with them. That task is to get them oriented to their new position. While this process will vary depending on the industry and specific environment, here are some key components to starting your new team member off right:

> **Specify a Start Time** – I can't tell you how often I have seen new employees show up bright and early to make a great first impression, and then have to sit and wait with nothing to do until their manager arrives. Don't just specify a start date, set a time (I usually use 10AM) for the new hire to get started. This gives you a chance to get in and put out any fires, prepare paperwork and generally get yourself ready to greet the newest member of the team.

> **Have a Team Lunch** – It's great to have an informal forum for your new hire to meet the members of their team. This doesn't have to be an expensive or fancy meal; you can just sit together in the cafeteria or meet over sandwiches in a conference room.

> **Provide Space and Tools** – Be sure you know where your new team member is going to sit, and make sure they have whatever they need in place on day one. This may mean communicating with the IT department to ensure that usernames and passwords are set up, and that equipment gets issued.

➤ **Create a Schedule** – For the first week you may want to build out a schedule for getting this individual ramped up. They will need to meet with Human Resources, and you will probably want to make some time on your schedule to give them a more detailed picture of how the department operates. Finally you will want to provide dedicated time for them to spend with specific members of the group to get up to speed on projects or processes that they need to know.

Hiring great people is a key component of having a successful team. If you are a cook, you know that the quality of your ingredients has a direct effect on the quality of the final dish. Use care and judgment when you are looking to add a new member to your team and pay close attention to their experience as they come on board. These steps will ensure that you start your relationship off on the right foot, and maximize the potential for successfully integrating your new employee into the team.

CHAPTER 15

Building a Business Case

Your team is up and running and you have identified some key short and long term initiatives. Often the pursuit of these initiatives will be made more effective by investing in new tools, more staff, or training. You can't just go out and buy what you think you need – your manager and possibly the finance group will need to approve any spending that you do.

In the past you probably asked your direct manager for whatever tool you wanted, and they told you whether or not you could get it. Now that you are the manager, you will need to weigh the cost of these new initiatives against the value that they bring to your team or your organization. You will then present that analysis to your manager and/or upper management in order to secure approval for the initiative.

There are two primary factors which will influence whether or not the requests you make will be approved.

1. **Your Budget** – If this is an item such as training or a tool purchase that you anticipated (or your manager anticipated) during the budgeting cycle, you may be able to move forward with the purchase immediately.

2. **Value to the Organization** – Some initiatives will have an immediate and tangible benefit to the organization. For example, hiring another staff member might allow you to deliver more service, for which you currently lack the capacity. You can make a case for your new hire based on the idea that it won't cost the company money, but instead will allow your group to generate more revenue.

Building a business case is not as hard as it sounds. In many organizations the process is informal for smaller initiatives, but you will still need to articulate the costs and benefits of what you want to do. Business justifications generally fall into one of three major categories:

- Risk Management
- Operational Efficiency
- Competitive Advantage

RISK MANAGEMENT

Risk Management is a process of measuring potential negative implications to the organization, and developing solutions to manage their impact. Some common tactics for risk management include transferring the risk to another party, avoiding the risk, reducing the negative effect of the risk, and accepting some or all of the consequences of a particular risk.

In practical terms, this means that the executives and decision makers in an organization must make numerous decisions regarding how and on what to spend money. These decisions are usually a delicate balance of trying to minimize spending on the operational processes of the organization as opposed to investing in initiatives that are likely to increase revenue and profitability.

The need to implement any solution is measured by the cost of the risk it is designed to mitigate. In an ideal world we (and business executives) would be able to easily identify and quantify both the tangible and intangible impact of every risk, and then have a very precise and isolated dollar figure to benchmark how that risk should be addressed. In practice, however, this is very difficult to achieve. Your goal in building a business case based on risk management is to provide an accurate assessment of the impact of the risk in contrast to the cost and probability of avoiding the risk through implementing the solution you propose.

OPERATIONAL EFFICIENCY

Operational Efficiency is another valid business justification for making an investment. Initiatives in this category aim to drive value to the business through saving time and money, enhancing productivity, and focusing efforts on business-critical services. Operational efficiency includes these business benefits:

- Cost control
- Consistency of service delivery
- Reduction of administrative overhead
- Improved scalability and adaptability to support the business though change

Initiatives that relate to improving the operational efficiency of the organization include the purchase of software tools, training, hiring staff, etc. These purchases are designed to provide business value by reducing the cost of a portion of the operations of the organization. Here's a basic example from the manufacturing industry.

In a manufacturing environment, a machine might be placed on the production line that can turn out 10 times as many widgets as a person can make manually. If this machine costs $500,000, and the person it replaces costs $30,000/year, the cost justification would look like this:

- The machine costs $500,000 over 5 years or $100,000/year

- The Employee costs $30,000/year
- Output of widgets with machine = 100/hour
- Output of widgets with employee = 10/hour
- Each widget earns the company $1

If you assume that the machine operates for the same number of hours that the person would work, you can figure out how many widgets each one produces over the course of the year:

- Machine = 100 widgets x 40 hours x 50 weeks = 200,000/year
- Person = 10 widgets x 40 hours x 50 weeks = 20,000/year

The machine will produce 100x52x5x8 widgets/year or $200,000 worth of widgets per year while the person will produce $20,000. So the machine will have paid for itself in 2.5 years, whereas the person costs the company $10,000 per year.

This type of return on investment calculation is easy to analyze and understand. The costs are fixed, and the return is easily measured in greater productivity and profitability. Obviously in the real world there are variables even to this simple equation that would make it more complex. Can the machine be used 24x7? If so the profit is more. Are there expenditures beyond the cost of the machine related to electricity, repair, maintenance, or facilities upgrades that are required? If so the profit is less. These costs also have to be factored into the potential business value.

To make an Operational Efficiency based business case for an initiative you need to be able to answer the following questions:

1. How much does the system cost in total (including implementation, training, hardware, support/maintenance, etc.)?
2. What employees does the system affect?
3. How much time does it save them in comparison to their current process?
4. How does that affect the organization (Can they process more orders with fewer people)?
5. Is there a tangible cost savings to the organization (reduction in number of workstations to be purchased, reduction in usage of utilities or physical space requirements, etc.)?

COMPETITIVE ADVANTAGE

Competitive Advantage based justifications can actually be considered an aspect of Risk Management or Operational Efficiency as well. One aim of a business justification based on competitive advantage is to mitigate the risk that customers might decide to take their business elsewhere due to a competitor having a better process or product. A trading organization's ability to tout their internal infrastructure as having passed a security audit with flying colors, for example, might gain them a competitive advantage over a competing firm which has not been audited and/or cannot be audited due to an insecure configuration.

Alternatively, you can propose an initiative based on the competitive advantage you will receive from improving your internal processes. Hiring more customer service agents will improve the response times for handling customer calls, and thus provide better service to new and existing customers.

Of the three potential justifications, this one is the most difficult to directly prove through cost/benefit analysis due to the fact that the benefits are often unknown or difficult to measure. The amount of business lost to a competitor will probably be tracked by the Sales Department, but their ability to gain quality insights from clients who have switched to a competitor about exactly why they chose to leave can be challenging. Additionally, it is difficult (if not impossible) to tell where those clients went.

In most cases where a competitive advantage based case is being made, it is because a competitor has already made an investment in a new technology. Other organizations are feeling pressured to make the same investment to be perceived as equal by their customers.

No matter which of the business justification methods you choose, you will need to make sure that your case is supported by facts and thorough analysis. In the early months of your tenure as a manager, neither your manager nor the finance department will have experience with your judgment. Because of this lack of history they will want to see the facts and figures behind your requests.

As you build relationships with these individuals, as well as others within your organization, they will (hopefully) learn to trust that you have done your homework, and would not recommend an initiative that had no intrinsic value to the organization. The more thoroughly you research and support your initial presentations, the more quickly you will be seen as someone who is conscious of building business value.

CHAPTER 16

Running Effective Meetings

As a manager you will spend time meeting with many people. You will certainly meet with your team members, individually as well as in a group, but you will also spend time with your management team, your vendors, and your customers. While meetings are a fundamental part of business life, they are often poorly structured and result in a lot of discussion but little action. Your goal, therefore, is to manage your meetings to maximize the benefit both you and your team members receive from taking time out of your busy days to get together. The requirements for a successful meeting are as follows:

> ➤ Enforce Business Etiquette
> ➤ Have an Agenda
> ➤ Have a "Parking Lot"
> ➤ Take Notes and Send a Follow Up Email

ETIQUETTE

There are several fundamental pieces of meeting etiquette that, as a manager, you will need to enforce and as a meeting attendee you will need to adhere to.

Laptops/Mobile Devices

Many of your colleagues (probably yourself included) will have laptops and mobile devices such as phones with internet access as tools to help you be more productive. The temptation to pop open your laptop and work on other things during a meeting can be over-whelming. It is also highly counterproductive to the effectiveness of the meeting. Set up guidelines at your first meeting regarding the use of laptops, answering of phone calls, and sending of text messages during meetings.

While there are some circumstances where someone has to take a call (parents of small children, sales people waiting on a big deal to close, etc.), for the most part, all phones should be on vibrate, and all laptops should be closed with the exception of the person taking notes. If it's a working meeting where everyone has to have a file open or needs access to email or the internet, make sure everyone is clear that no other tasks should be performed during that time period.

Start On-Time

As an individual contributor you might have a handful of administrative meetings per week (this does not count meetings you attend as part of your production such as sales presentations if you are a salesperson). As a manager, you and the majority of your fellow managers will spend a large percentage of your time in meetings. Because meetings are often scheduled back to back, it's a serious inconvenience to start meetings late or have them run beyond their scheduled end time.

You will probably attend meetings run by others that don't start or end when they are supposed to. There is not much you can do about that. Where your own meetings are concerned, you should make every effort to begin and end at your published meeting times. That may mean starting before everyone has arrived. While that may annoy some late-comers initially, it will teach people that your meetings begin when they are scheduled to begin. In the future people will arrive on time.

Sample Meeting Agenda

Meeting Title: Customer Service Weekly Staff Meeting
Location: Conference Room C
Date: Thursday, November 11th 2010
Time: 10:00-11:00 AM

Topic	Owner	Category	Time Limit
New Customer Info	Katy	FYI	10 minutes
Idea for New Product	Mike	Discussion	20 minutes
Update on Client Meetings	Sarah	FYI	15 minutes
Presentation from HR	Beth	FYI	15 minutes

Detailed Topic Information

- **New Customer Info** – Katy will be presenting a brief summary of the new major client that was signed last week. They have some specific needs in terms of response times and service level agreements that everyone needs to be aware of.

- **Idea for New Product** – Mike was asked to research options for updating our existing product vs. creating something new. He will be presenting his ideas and market research to the group.

- **Update on Client Meetings** – Sarah has been conducting meetings with our clients to gather information about how they feel about our customer service. She will be presenting her findings in this meeting.

- **Presentation from Human Resources** – Beth, from Human Resources will be presenting more information on the new benefits package. She will then be available for individual questions after the meeting

Have an Agenda

Every meeting should have an agenda that's published in advance. You want your team to be able to come prepared with relevant information, questions and comments in order to get the most out of the time you spend together. Each item on the agenda should be categorized into one of the following groups:

FYI/Update

Items in this category will be one-way announcements with no expectation that a follow up discussion will take place in the current meeting. If team members have questions or want more information, ask them to schedule a time to meet with you separately, or place it on the agenda for the next meeting as a discussion.

If you know (or suspect) that a particular item is going to be contentious or require follow up, take the proactive step of scheduling a separate time for discussion. For example if Human Resources announces a change in the health insurance options and asks you to give the information to your team, you can anticipate that there will be questions. You should request that a member of the Human Resources team comes at a separately scheduled time to address any questions or concerns, or get a point of contact for your team members to meet with individually to discuss the full impact of the change.

Correctly categorizing these items will prevent you and your team from wasting time discussing issues which have already been decided.

Discussion

Any time that you or another team member wants to solicit information from the team it should be listed as a discussion. Discussions should always have time limits. Let's say that you are running a software development team, and one of your senior developers has an idea for a new product. He wants to put it out to the team, run through his methodology in developing the concept, and see if anyone has any ideas or resources that could help him. That's a great topic for discussion and will allow him to leverage the knowledge of his team members to be more efficient!

With a discussion, there is no expectation that a decision will be reached in the meeting. A time limit is necessary otherwise discussions have a tendency to go on for extended periods of time. Allow 10-20 minutes for people to toss out ideas. Make sure that you (or the person who requested the discussion agenda item) take notes and record what comes up. Then let people know that they can follow up with any other thoughts after the meeting.

Decision

At times you will need to make a decision in a meeting based on information you gather from your team members. While you can present it as a discussion topic in one meeting to get your team's feedback, and then present the decision as an FYI/Announcement at a later date, it is more efficient for quick decisions to be made within the timeframe of a single session with your staff.

It may be helpful to use a decision framework if you are trying to reach consensus with a group of people. These tools allow you to articulate the issue at hand, the results you seek, the options for resolution, and ultimately, to make a decision. The first key to successful decision making is to clearly define the problem you are trying to solve. A tool that I find useful is the IROD framework which was first introduced to me by Tom Lippie, President of Client First Associates. IROD is an acronym for the following:

- Issue
- Results
- Options
- Decision

This framework describes an outline for bringing a group to consensus. Using a whiteboard or other large writing space, you can walk your team through defining the issue, articulating the desired results, brainstorming options, and finally choosing a path forward from the available options. The tool works because it allows you to define the results you seek. It is then easy to see which options will achieve those results. It's hard enough to reach consensus when everyone agrees on the results they seek. It's almost impossible if there is disagreement on that point.

Table 7 - IROD Framework

ISSUE	Define, as specifically as possible, the nature of the issue or problem to be resolved. Include the impact on business or the department.
RESULTS	Brainstorm the results required and any desired outcomes from the decision you will make to resolve this issue.
OPTIONS	List all options for resolving this issue. This should be an open discussion – don't make judgments until all of the options are on the table.
DECISION	Choose one or more of the options which is most likely to produce the required results.

As an example of how the IROD tool can be used to facilitate a decision, let's consider a challenge facing a customer service team:

Issue: Customers are hanging up because they have to wait too long on hold before they are connected with someone who can help them.

Impact: Loss of revenue – dissatisfied customers are switching their business to another vendor which has put the churn rate (the number of customers per month who cancel their service) over the target rate.

Required Results: Upper management approval that losing these customers is acceptable if we maintain status quo OR reduction of hold time for customers so they don't hang up.

Potential Solutions:

1. Present case to upper management that customer service is understaffed – get approval for more customer service agents or approval for higher acceptable churn rate.
2. Change the process for handling calls to reduce the time on hold.
3. Train customer service agents so that calls can be resolved faster.
4. Leverage engineering department to field complex calls that exceed the standard average time limit.

Decision: Based on information from agents, there is no process change or training that would substantially impact the time on hold metric. Therefore the team leader will work with engineering to see if calls of a specific level can be handed off to engineers rather than customer service agents. If this does not resolve the issue or is not possible, the team leader will present the case for hiring more customer service agents to upper management.

By using this process you will accomplish several key goals. First, by clearly articulating the issue at hand, you will focus the discussion on the specifics of the situation. By stating your desired results (and framing it alongside the business impact) you can eliminate any potential solutions that would not achieve those results. Finally, by allowing for multiple possible solutions, you can choose to pursue one, some, or all of the options on the table.

Building consensus within your team on how to solve a particular issue can be a complex process. Some discussions may become heated or people may disagree strongly. Your primary role in the facilitation of meetings, particularly when decisions must be made, is to enforce respectful communication between team members, and to keep everyone focused on the goal. If topics come up that are outside the bounds of the discussion, they should be placed in the "Parking Lot" (which we are about to discuss) to be covered at another time.

As with discussions, decisions should have time limits. If you feel you are not close to a decision after 90% of the time has gone by, inform the team members that you will record the results of the discussion and, if the decision is time sensitive, determine what solution will be implemented yourself. If there is no time constraint and you feel that there is value in continuing the discussion, or if a piece of information is required to continue the process productively, you can also put it on the agenda for a future meeting.

The goal of this process is not to achieve 100% consensus. It will be a rare occasion that every member of your team agrees with what you choose. By having a collaborative decision making process, you will allow everyone to be heard. You may also uncover options you would not have thought of on your own and you will know where each member of your team stands on the issue.

The Parking Lot

A "Parking Lot" is exactly what it sounds like – a place to table issues for future discussion. Many times a discussion will evolve from its initial topic into another subject entirely. While that topic may be valid and important, if it was not part of the agenda it can take away valuable time from the relevant discussion of the original item. Whenever you feel that a discussion has gone off topic, write it down and suggest that it should be discussed separately at another time.

If you have a white board in your conference room you should start off your meeting by drawing a box in one of the upper corners and labeling it "Parking Lot". This will help your team learn the habit of tabling off-topic discussions, and keep the schedule on track.

TAKE NOTES AND SEND A FOLLOW UP

Years ago, when departments all had secretaries, you could expect someone else to take notes, send meeting minutes around, and generally maintain the administrative processes of your group. Today, with the prevalence of technology in the workplace, support staff levels have dropped significantly. Unless you are a high level executive (in which case I doubt very much that you would be reading this book), you will be responsible for keeping track of what happens in your meetings, and sending out notes and action items to your team.

Taking notes does not mean recording every word that's spoken at a meeting. In fact, if you spend all of your time writing down what's being said, you will be completely unable to facilitate the meeting. Your best bet is to use your original agenda, and jot down any results or action items from each item. Ideally, your team members will all be paying strict attention in meetings and will note down any action items that require their individual attention. In practice if you have not documented the action items you will be hearing lots of excuses for why things didn't get done.

Any time an actionable item comes up in a meeting it should be assigned to a team member and a timeline should be associated with it. That way, you can follow up to ensure that people are moving forward with their deliverables, and everyone will clearly understand their own responsibilities.

CHAPTER 17

Dealing with Conflict

No matter how prepared you are for your new role – how many management books your read, training seminars you attend, or new skills you learn – you will have moments where you feel completely overwhelmed and unprepared for your new job.

Last year we adopted a 6 month old puppy from a shelter. As a family, we decided it was time to bring another dog into our household as our current family pet (a 13 year old lab/Dalmatian) was getting towards the end of her days. When we brought Prima home, we were thrilled and excited to have a new member of the family. I am a mother, a successful consultant, and have raised a dog before. I had a leash, food, treats, training and a crate. I had every expectation that after a few weeks of training, she would be the perfect dog.

Three weeks later I was convinced that I had made the worst decision of my life. She chewed up my socks, threw up on the rug, jumped on my son, peed in the house, pulled on the leash, and generally behaved like… well, like a 6 month old puppy. I had forgotten how long it took and how hard we worked with our first dog to get her to the point where she understood her role in the household, and did what we asked of her. A year later Prima is a fully integrated member of our family. While she has her own quirks and personality issues, the communication flow is much improved and I am back to feeling competent again.

When you are comfortable in a role, it can be easy to forget the challenges you went through to get to that point. Transitioning to a new position, developing communication channels with a team when you have never managed before, and possibly evolving from a peer to a team leader is a huge change. You can expect to face some challenges in your first weeks and months as a leader. In this chapter we will explore some obstacles you may encounter and some tools you can use when challenges arise – whether they come from your team members, customers and colleagues, or whether they come from inside of yourself.

CHALLENGES FROM YOUR TEAM

In all likelihood, you were not the only person in contention for this management position when you were hired. In fact, if you are new to the organization, there was probably someone internal to the company who was hoping to get your job as a promotion. If you were promoted from within there may have been other people within the organization and even within your own team who aspired to your job.

Most businesses are internally competitive by nature. Very few people expect to stay in one position for their entire careers, and so there is a constant undercurrent of opportunity awareness throughout any medium to large organization. While you cannot prevent the possibility that hard feelings may exist because someone felt they deserved the position more than you do, you can control how you respond to that scenario.

Feelings about being passed over for a promotion are only one of the reasons that someone might have a poor attitude towards their job. When you walk into a new management position, you are inheriting an ecosystem of individuals and their personal lives, recent (and sometimes not so recent) experiences within the organization, and overall morale. While you may feel like you are starting with a clean slate, it's likely that there are some residual challenges which comes with the territory. Uncovering and dealing with these issues early on in your tenure will avoid their festering and growing into large scale problems later.

A bad attitude is hard to hide. In all likelihood, during your individual meetings in Week 3, you uncovered someone on your team who doesn't love their job, and may be openly or covertly hostile towards you and your position. Here are some strategies you can use to surface and defuse negativity within your group:

1. **Consider Personality** – Before you decide that an individual is not an enthusiastic supporter, consider their natural personality. If you are a raging extrovert and you have a team member who is more introverted and analytical, it's likely that it's a personal communication style issue. There are many personality and communication style assessments available. It can be helpful to use one or more of these to gain insight into the individual styles of your team, and to communicate effectively with them. See the Resources section for more information.

2. **Wait and Observe** – While first impressions are often accurate, your team member may just be having a bad day. Use your first impression as an indication that you should pay close attention to the actions and words of this individual. After a couple of weeks of observation if you still see and feel hostility, it's time to move on to option 3.

3. **Speak Privately** – Find a non-stressful time to meet one on one with your team member and see if you can uncover the root of the issue. Using the tools we have discussed in earlier chapters, try to ascertain whether this is an employee with a motivation issue, skill issue, or some other underlying frustration with the organization as a whole. Approach the conversation in a positive way and actively seek to understand the problem rather than trying to fix it on the spot or blowing it up into a confrontation. Use the structured

decision process from Chapter 12, if it seems appropriate, to try to facilitate a resolution. You might be surprised at how quickly people become your allies when you make it clear that they are important and valuable members of your team.

4. **Engage Human Resources** – If the previous options don't work, don't let it fester until you have a larger morale problem on your team. Engage your Human Resources Department. Describe the issue, and ask for help in bringing about a resolution. Many organizations have a structured process for dealing with employee issues and it will help your credibility as a manager to work within the system to get the help you need. If this is the first time you have dealt with true conflict resolution, having the support of someone who has been through it before can help you approach the situation with confidence.

5. **Don't Take It Personally** – While an individual's negative attitude might make you frustrated and angry at times, it is important to keep the entire process professional. Your role is to create an environment which supports and encourages individual success. If someone chooses not to work within that system after you have made a concerted effort to uncover and resolve any obstacles to their success, you have to keep your cool, communicate that information clearly and

move on to managing the people who do want to work with you.

Research into why employees choose to change jobs has shown that there is a clear link between the relationship an individual has with their manager, and their overall satisfaction with their job. It follows that a change in management can be a worrisome thing for many people.

Since it has the potential for such a direct and personal impact, some people experience anxiety and concern during this time of transition. Ideally if you follow the plan articulated in this book, and build your management and leadership skills, your team members will adapt to the change quickly and this anxiety level will be reduced.

CHALLENGES FROM YOUR ORGANIZATION

Growing up, I always thought that companies were run by experienced people who knew exactly what they were doing. It wasn't until I held my first management job that I had a glimpse into the changeable, sometimes disjointed and occasionally incomprehensible world of business management. While there are some companies that operate in a perfectly streamlined and flawless manner, the majority do not.

Depending on how large your organization is, and where you fit in the grand scheme of things, you may or may not be privy to the executive level conversations and meetings which result in the high level goals and objectives of the organization. But whether or not you actually see inside of those meetings, you will feel their impact as goals and objectives are pushed down through the organization.

Earlier in this book, we talked about aligning your goals with the objectives of the company as a whole. While that will be your intent, you may find that those larger goals are sometimes moving targets. It can be frustrating to spend weeks or months working diligently in one direction, only to discover that upper management has a made a strategic decision to eliminate that objective or change it in some way that materially impacts what you have done to date.

The temptation when this happens (and unfortunately it will) is to get mad, to vent to your staff or your colleagues, and to feel frustrated about all of that lost effort. While it may make you feel better at the time, getting worked up about things you can't control will undermine your ability to steer your team through these challenges, especially when changes like these are common in most organizations. Your best bet is to keep your cool, keep your team informed, and adjust your course.

One key thing you should not do when objectives change is throw away the work you've done. Projects that get tabled or put on the back burner for a period of time have a tendency of coming back around. Make sure you archive and document any work you have done towards an objective so that you can come back to it later if you need to. That way you'll have a head start on the next change and won't be doubly frustrated by having to re-do work you have already done.

CHALLENGES FROM YOUR CUSTOMERS

Often customers, both internal and external will see a newly promoted manager as someone who might not yet know the ropes. You may find some folks who will try to take advantage of that by attempting to re-negotiate existing arrangements, ask for something they couldn't get before, or in some way test your mettle. One of the important reasons to go through the 90 Day Action Plan is to make sure you have done your homework on your customers early on in the process.

Ideally, before you have your first interaction with your customers, you will have had the opportunity to review existing contracts, get to know the customer's history with the organization, and understand what latitude you have in making deals. But it's possible that someone will slip in early and try to make changes before you have a full grasp of how things operate.

Your best bet in avoiding this type of challenge is (with the support of your own manager) to create a policy that no changes will be made to existing contracts and procedures in the first 90 days. This will give you time to ramp up your relationship with your team, orient yourself within the organization, and get your feet under you. If you can defer all changes until after you have completed your first 90 days, you will be in a far better position to understand the impact those changes will have on your team over the long run, and to avoid making mistakes.

FINDING SOLUTIONS

One of the key traits of a great manager is their ability to get things done despite whatever obstacles arise. You've heard the descriptive terms so often they probably don't mean much to you anymore:

> ➤ Self Starter
> ➤ Self Motivated
> ➤ Results Oriented

In practice, what all of these terms describe is a person who takes an objective and runs with it. When they encounter obstacles, they find ways around, over or through them. To boil it down to a very short analogy, my first mentor told me that if I encountered a problem that prevented me from getting my work done, I should always come up with three options on how to overcome the obstacle before I went to my manager for help. It's good advice for an individual contributor, but it's even better advice for a manager.

How do you come up with three solutions when you are stuck? Here are some places to look before you go knock on your manager's door:

1. **Reach Out** – Back in Chapter 2 we talked about how to figure out what's expected of you in your new role, and I mentioned joining networking groups in your field or industry. It can be helpful to toss a challenge or problem out to your

networking group and see if anyone has run into it before.

2. **Take a Walk** – I get my best ideas from walking away from a problem for a while. While this may not work if you are under a tight deadline, it's an excellent solution for longer term issues. Put the problem aside and go for a run, take a walk, work on something else entirely or go get a cup of coffee. Your brain doesn't forget the problem. It keeps on working it while you work on something else and you may be surprised at the flashes of inspiration that come to you about one thing when you are focused on something entirely different.

3. **Explain it to Someone Else** – When you describe a problem to someone else, you may find that you look at it in a new way and see an option you didn't see before. If describing it to a friend or colleague doesn't help, the business world is full of consultants and experts in every possible field. While you may not have the budget for a full analysis, most consultants will come in, listen to your description of the issue and work up a proposal with a cost estimate to solve the problem and some options on how to get it done. While it's not a solution in and of itself, it's a resource and a budget number that you can put before your manager as an option.

4. **Search the Web** – The internet contains a wealth of information – sometimes so much that it can be challenging to mine through all of the dirt to find the nuggets of gold. Answers are out there and you will often find inspiration or options you hadn't considered just by searching. When in doubt, type your problem into your favorite search engine phrased as a question and see what comes up.

You will find that there are many demands on your time in your new role, and your direct manager is probably just as burdened. Your goal is overcome as many obstacles as you can on your own. When you are completely stuck, make sure you come to the conversation prepared with all of the facts about the situation so you can make the best use of your manager's time.

Momentum Wrap Up

As you build on the success of your first 90 days, you will encounter many challenges. It is beyond the scope of this book to cover all of the skills you will need to learn in order to be successful. Every successful manager (and person for that matter) that I know is committed to a process of continuous improvement.

Actively seek out new resources when you encounter challenges in your career. When I was in college I was a member of the crew team. The following words were stenciled in large letters on the wall of our workout room:

Pain is Weakness Leaving the Body

I have no doubt that you will encounter struggles in the course of your tenure as a manager, but if you can view them as opportunities to learn and grow, you will be on the right track. In the following (and final) section of this book I have listed some resources to help you find more information on the topics discussed here, as well as other areas to explore as you develop in your new career.

Resources

Throughout this book I have discussed the need to adopt an attitude of continuous improvement as it relates to your professional development. In this section I have compiled a list of tools and resources for you to use as a jumping off point. This is by no means a comprehensive list, but I have included some of the major players in each area. Included in this section are:

- Suggested Reading - Books
- Time Management Training Providers
- Leadership Training Providers
- Communication Style and Personality Assessment Tools
- Performance Management and Evaluation Tools

As part of your personal development plan, you will want to put together a library of books and reference materials that help you stay on track. In this section I have listed books, time management solutions, seminars and web sites that will serve as a starting point in your personal development plan. These resources are industry standard tools and references which you will probably hear referenced by your management colleagues.

In addition to the resources provided in this section, I post and maintain reference materials and supplemental information at www.surviveyourpromotion.com. If you have purchased this book you are eligible to receive a free download of the tools and templates referenced in the text. Please visit the web site to learn how to access your free management toolkit.

SUGGESTED READING - BOOKS

The 7 Habits of Highly Effective People
Stephen R. Covey
Free Press, 2004

How to Win Friends and Influence People
Dale Carnegie
Simon & Schuster, 2009

The 21 Irrefutable Laws of Leadership: Follow Them and People Will Follow You
John C. Maxwell
Thomas Nelson, 2007

The One Minute Manager
Kenneth Blanchard, PhD. and Spencer Johnson, M.D.
William Morrow, 1982

The Five Dysfunctions of a Team
Patrick Lencioni
Jossey-Bass, A Wiley Company, 2002

The Trusted Advisor
David H. Maister, Charles H. Green and Robert M. Galford
Free Press, 2001

First, Break all the Rules: What the World's Greatest Managers Do Differently
Marcus Buckingham and Curt Coffman
Simon & Schuster, 1999

Raving Fans: A Revolutionary Approach to Customer Service
Ken Blanchard and Sheldon Bowles
William Morrow, 1993

The 10 Natural Laws of Successful Time and Life Management
Hyrum W. Smith
Business Plus, 1995

Five Management Principles in One CREAD: A Management Guide to Live By
James Lippie
iUniverse Inc., 2004

TIME MANAGEMENT TRAINING PROVIDERS

Each of the sites listed below provide training in time management, leadership, and general management techniques. These are great resources if you want to build on a specific skill, or learn about a topic in more depth.

Franklin-Covey Time Management System
www.franklincovey.com

David Allen's GTD (Get Things Done) System
www.davidco.com

Pomodoro Technique
www.pomodorotechnique.com

The Project Management Institute
PMP (Project Management Professional) Certification
www.pmi.org

LEADERSHIP TRAINING PROVIDERS

As we discussed in Part 1, leadership and management are related but separate skills. The goal of management is primarily to plan, organize and implement processes to get things done. Leadership is the act of inspiring others to perform at a higher level. Truly effective managers have strong leadership skills, and leadership training can be a key component of your personal development plan. Here are some organizations that provide leadership training:

The Dale Carnegie Institute
www.dalecarnegie.com

Client First Associates
www.clientfirstassociates.com

The Center for Management and Organizational Effectiveness (CMOE)
www.cmoe.com/leadership-training.htm

American Management Association
www.amanet.org

COMMUNICATION AND PERSONALITY ASSESSMENT TOOLS

As with time management, there are many tools and instruments to assess communication style and personality. Each of the sites listed below describes a type of tool and will allow you to find practitioners who can deliver it to your staff and help you interpret the results. In most cases you can take a sample assessment online and see a summary of the results. I recommend that you try each one and see what fits the needs of your team and your organization.

Most Human Resources managers are familiar with these tools, and may be able to tell you which ones have been used in the organization in the past. They may even be certified in the use of a specific assessment, so start with an email or conversation with your Human Resources Department for guidance on this process.

Myers Briggs
www.myersbriggs.org

Margerison-McCann Team Management Profile
www.tmsdi.com

Kiersey Temperment Scale
www.kiersey.com

The Forté Institute
www.theforteinstitute.com

PERFORMANCE MANAGEMENT AND EVALUATION TOOLS

Your first step in evaluating employee performance is your Human Resources Department if there is one. In smaller organizations this function is often provided through the Finance Department and on occasion a consultant or other outsourced provider does the work of Human Resources. It is highly unlikely that you will be asked to create your own performance evaluation forms, or to make up new evaluation processes as a new manager. However, it can be helpful to understand what other organizations do, since some of their tools and templates can give you ideas for keeping track of your own employee's performance.

Society for Human Resource Management
http://www.shrm.org
This industry group provides tools and resources to Human Resources professionals. They offer a wide variety of articles and information on employee relations and legal issues related to human resource management. Their tools and templates directory is a member's only area, but many parts of the site are accessible to anyone.

Microsoft Corporation
http://office.microsoft.com/
The Microsoft Office Suite™ is a commonly used set of business applications, which you may currently use. Their website has a wealth of downloadable tools and templates including review forms.

Human Resources Village

http://www.hrvillage.com/hrtoolkit.htm

This site provides articles, templates, and other resources for people dealing with employee relations and other Human Resources topics.

Salary.com

http://www.salary.com

Salary and total compensation information can vary from market to market. This site provides information on compensation packages for a wide variety of industries and job titles.

About the Author

Katy Tynan has spent more than 15 years in the IT industry, both as an individual contributor and a manager. As the Director of Consulting and Compliance Services for Thrive Networks, she created a business unit which provided strategic consulting to small and medium businesses throughout the Northeast. Founder of Personal Focus Coaching, Katy currently provides coaching services to individuals and organizations who seek to enhance the performance of their key employees and to develop the leadership skills of newly promoted managers. For more management tips and resources, please visit the Survive Your Promotion blog at http://surviveyourpromotion.com.

Made in the USA
Lexington, KY
04 September 2010